P. JOHN BRUNSTETTER, PHD

IT ONLY HURTS WHEN I
LISTEN

*Using radical listening to transform
your listening & your life*

IT ONLY HURTS WHEN I LISTEN

By P. John Brunstetter

Publisher's Acknowledgements:
A special thank you to all the individuals who assisted in the creation of this publication:

Proofreader: Kirstin Cornfield
Editorial Assistant: Alicia Whitecavage
Project Editor: Thomas Floyd Marshall
Editorial Manager: Sarah Funderburke
Layout and Graphics: Hannah Coward

ISBN: 978-1-935986-25-6

http://www.ItOnlyHurtsWhenIListen.com

LIBERTY
U N I V E R S I T Y.
Press

Lynchburg, Va.
www.liberty.edu/libertyuniversitypress

THE
RADICAL LISTENERS' PLEDGE ©

I WILL SHOW OTHERS HOW MUCH I CARE BY HOW I LISTEN TO THEM:

- I will ask others to speak first as often as possible
- I will keep my mouth shut and my ears, mind and heart wide open
- I will listen with a sincere desire to be influenced
- I will respond to others with an encouraging spirit

TABLE OF CONTENTS

FOREWORD
KEN BLANCHARD
Coauthor of *The One Minute Manager*®₁ and *The Servant Leader*

For years I have been a passionate pioneer in championing servant leadership, because I believe it is the only way to lead effectively. While we have done a good job of encouraging leaders to be humble servants of those they lead, we have not thoroughly emphasized the performance potential of servant "listening." *It Only Hurts When I Listen* shows how and why servant listening improves ROL (Return on Listening) not just for leaders but for everyone.

In his *Ten Principles of Servant Leadership,*² my friend Larry Spears lays the foundation for all servant leadership by describing listening as the first of the 10 fundamental servant leadership characteristics. *It Only Hurts When I Listen* takes Larry's Principal #1 to a richer, more radical level by showing us how to listen with a servant's heart.

In our book *The Servant Leader,*³ Phil Hodges and I describe the different leadership styles that are required to direct and support subordinates. We contend that the ability to listen well is critical to effective servant leadership. *It Only Hurts When I Listen* builds on this theme by pointing out that effective listening begins with the "unnatural" ability to understand and speak in the communication language of others. This situational listening is necessary if we are to truly serve the people in our lives. Making meaningful changes to how we listen may at times be messy, painful, and difficult, but in the end it is well worth the effort.

In Chapter 15 of this book I share my thoughts about servant listening using my own communication language i.e., as a Flexible/Adapter. I hope you are inspired by how my dad and others impacted my servant leadership and servant listening. In Chapters 9–15 you will see how Richard Blackaby, Mike Freeman, Rob Jackson and the Colonel respectively practice radical servant listening using completely different communication languages than mine. You will also have a chance to discover your own communication style and more importantly, you'll learn how to better recognize and respond to others by using their listening language.

By reading this book and applying what you learn about radical servant listening, you can strengthen every key relationship in your life. Your journey begins with an honest self-assessment of your listening behavior. You will then learn how to develop a servant's heart, as well as how you can overcome the root causes that underpin poor listening. Finally you will learn how to use the five communication languages to speak the truth in love with all those you serve. Love others – by listening to them!

INTRODUCTION

"Man's inability to communicate is a result of his failure to listen effectively."
— Carl Rogers [4]

Relationships at work and at home, with friends and with family are being undermined by poor listening at an unprecedented rate. Studies show that only 31 percent of American workers are actively engaged in their work.[5] Other studies show 50 percent of workers either dislike or distrust their boss.[6] Not surprisingly a recent Gallup poll shows that poor boss-subordinate interaction is the main reason people quit their jobs.[7] On the family front, divorce rate prognosticators suggest that 40-50 percent of people who marry today will be divorced within 10 years.[8] Single parent families appear to be on the rise and over 1 million children run away or are missing annually.[9] Why is our society running amok?

I suggest that the main reason for social unrest is escalating communication failure accelerated by poor listening. A new generation of "me first" millennials are extremely well-educated but increasingly more ineffective in verbal interaction. Poor listening has become viral because of their New Age dependency on electronics and social media and less and less on verbal interaction. Recent global economic meltdown has also changed the way we all think and how we communicate. We are becoming a culture of self-servicers with a strong need for instant gratification and less desire for social interaction. The need to listen effectively has become as devalued as the U.S. dollar. The need to express ourselves publicly and personally is what is now valued. Of all the things that have changed over the past 50 years I believe the one that is the most debilitating is that we have lost not only our ability to listen, but more critically, we have lost our *desire* to listen. The 2011 National Basketball Association (NBA) labor negotiations are a prime example of poor listening on both sides. The "Occupy Wall Street" demonstrations of 2011 in the U.S. and globally are another example of people saying to government "You are not listening to me!" Marriage and family counselors will confirm that addressing poor listening is where most therapy begins.

Tragically, the conditions above are just the tip of the social impact iceberg. The net effect of poor listening is underperformance and lack of fulfillment at every level of society especially in the workplace and in the family. Gallup polls also indicate that those who are dissatisfied with their immediate supervisor are 50 percent less productive and that the companies they work for are 45 percent less profitable than those with satisfying supervisory relationships.[10] The words highlighted below spoken in the movie *Cool Hand Luke* [11] sum up our current social condition quite accurately.

"What we have here is a failure to communicate."

The movie *Contagion* tracks the rapid progress of a lethal virus that kills everyone it contacts.[12] As the lethal pandemic grows, the worldwide medical community races to find an antidote for the virus and the panic that is spreading faster than the virus itself. After 40 years of study, action research, consulting and training in the communication battlefields I have no doubt that escalating poor and self-serving listening is a pandemic virus as deadly as Contagion. If left unchecked, poor and self-serving listening will systematically erode individuals, relationships, organizations, families and society.

It Only Hurts When I Listen identifies the surprising origins and hidden causes of poor listening. Also presented are a variety of radical antidotes to stimulate individuals, relationships and groups to heal and grow by becoming more "listening centric" and less "speaking centric." Invaluable contributions by Ken Blanchard, Richard Blackaby, Mike Freeman and others, deliver both a "wake up call" and customized "tool kit" for harnessing the transformative power of what we are now calling radical "servant listening." *It Only Hurts When I Listen* provides a simple and yet customized template for improving every individual, every relationship, every team, every family and every community using a unique and powerful approach to listening and communicating effectively.

After spending most of my early and mid-career helping people communicate I made a very disconcerting and troubling self-discovery. I was not a very good listener. I am embarrassed to admit that I had become a self-serving communicator focused mainly on what was in my own best interests. Unknowingly I had become dependent on and limited by electronic communication and my already poor listening skills had become worse. I also discovered that I had experienced significant physical hearing loss at the same time. After examining my life history, especially my failures, I came to the startling conclusion that most of the pain I have experienced and the pain I have inflicted on others was related in some way to poor listening.

Using my mid-career Ph.D. in Human and Organizational Development as a vehicle, I began digging deeper to learn how to overcome my own listening shortcomings. The deeper I went the more I realized that I was not alone as a dysfunctional and self-serving communicator.

Based on my doctoral research, post-doctoral work and work with tens of thousands of people, teams, companies and families here are three things I discovered:

1) Creating positive interpersonal chemistry is the key to the effectiveness of every relationship.
2) Effective "radical" listening is the key to building interpersonal trust, the critical foundation for interpersonal chemistry.
3) Given training in radical listening participants are able to build relationship trust, improve interpersonal chemistry and increase their fulfillment and performance.

Be aware: The approach we use to listening improvement is counter cultural i.e., we advocate "others first" and "what's in it for others" rather than the millennials mantra "What's in it for me?" Radical listening requires changes in attitude as well as behavior. The myriad of contemporary tools that claim to result in more effective listening focus exclusively on listening behavior, techniques and, in some cases, manipulative tricks. In this book you will learn how to overcome the root causes of your poor listening by shifting your listening paradigm as well as learning unique ways to improve your listening effectiveness. You will learn how to strengthen every relationship in your life for the long-term. This may appear to be a bold claim but with your commitment and persistence we intend to make it happen. Here is what you need to do:

1) Commit to discovering and then unlearning your "naturally poor" listening behaviors.
2) Develop a humble heart for becoming a radically effective listener.
3) Learn how to change your listening paradigm as well as your listening behavior.
4) Create a Radical Action Plan that includes learning to listen to others in their communication language as well as your own.

"We are more apt to change when the anticipated pleasure of our new behavior is significantly greater than the known pain of our current behavior."
— Philip Harvey "Doc" Brunstetter [13]

CHANGING LISTENING BEHAVIOR 101

The one common denominator in all sustained behavior change is that the new behavior must be perceived to be significantly better than the existing behavior. Improved listening is no exception. We will get motivated to change our listening paradigm and behavior if we anticipate something much better will be the result when we do. Traditional listening skill development has shown to be ineffective and disappointing. Sustained positive change involves a change of heart before our behavior can change. You are about to learn a new and more powerful listening paradigm that may appear to be over-the-top and impractical. That is why we continue to refer to it as "radical" servant listening. There is only one catch. You must be willing to stop your old and comfortable poor listening behaviors and replace them with new and initially uncomfortable behavior.

PERFECT PRACTICE

A few years ago I went to Fred, a golf teaching pro to get some help with my mediocre golf game. He asked me how long I had been playing, what I normally shot and how often I played? He then asked me to hit a few balls which I did. His next question I did not expect "How much effort are you prepared to put into improving your game?" I was puzzled and asked why that was important. His simple but profound answer was "John you have two significant flaws in your swing that cause you to be inconsistent in your swing. Based on my 30 years working with students there are two options for my helping you. If you will spend 1 session a week with me and a minimum of two hours a day on your game I will reconstruct your swing and help you eliminate those two flaws. If you work hard I believe we can get your swing turned around in about 60-90 days. Fred told me this was his "perfect practice makes perfect method." The alternative method if I was not going to invest the practice time was to help me compensate for my two flaws without significantly altering my current swing. He chided me that he called the latter his "minimal practice yields minimal results'" option. (He could have been conning me but he did say I could quit at any time and did not owe him anything additional. As it turns out he helped me reduce my golf index/ handicap by over five points in less than 90 days. And yes I took the radical perfect practice option.)

If you desire to improve your listening skills then you too have one of two choices to make just like I did with Fred my golf coach: (Radical) Perfect Practice or (Superficial) Minimal Practice. Either way you choose to respond this book will teach you some powerful "lessons" about listening. The effort you expend in learning and applying your new listening behavior in all parts of your life is up to you. Like Fred, I will begin by pointing out the natural listening flaws in your listening "swing." Then I will show you how to replace those flaws with highly proficient and more radical listening behavior. Again your degree of transformation depends on how much effort you will expend in learning how to listen well. More critically your future listening effectiveness depends on how radical you are to apply radical listening in relationships in your life using your new listening "swing."

PARADIGM SHIFTING

I hope you are able to change your listening improvement paradigm from a focus on steps, techniques and behaviors. Radical listening is a life-long and never ending "process" of continued growth. It's a way of life and living not a flavor of the month. Radical listening builds authentic, open, honest and mutually fulfilling relationships whether those relationships last only a few minutes or decades and an ongoing opportunity to "love on" others in a world where most people don't get "loved on" very much. In her book *Lead with LUV* Coleen Barrett, President Emeritus of Southwest Airlines and coauthor Ken Blanchard describe the need to create "LUVing" relationships with customers as well as with employees by listening to them and then empowering them.[14] (LUV is the New York Stock Exchange symbol for Southwest Airlines.) Coleen led her company to unprecedented growth and productivity by promoting servant listening with a "LUVing" heart at all levels of Southwest both inside and outside the company. This people strategy may seem a bit soft and touchy-feely but the bottom line results at Southwest for more than 20 years running show that servant listening is a "good and profitable business practice."

THANK YOU FROM THE BOTTOM OF MY SERVANT'S HEART

First of all I would like to thank my dad, Philip Harvey Brunstetter, or "Doc" as we called him, for his lifelong mentoring and coaching. To this day he is still the best executive and leadership coach I have ever observed in action. Most of what I know and use today in human and organizational development I learned from Doc long before I ever learned it from a textbook, lecture or class. Doc was a pioneer in our field and as a tribute to him I promised on his deathbed that I would document what he taught me for others to use to transform their relationships.

Dr. Malcolm Knowles has influenced me greatly with his teaching on Adult Learning. He showed me that adults listen and learn differently than children, due to their desire to apply what they already know to solving day-to-day problems. Malcolm taught me to KISS when teaching adults (Keep It Short and Simple).

I want to thank Guy Baker, a financial and wealth planning guru and friend, for his tireless persistence in listening to me and forcing me to improve my own listening and writing behaviors. Enzo Calamo my "Canadian" connection, "Coach" Mike Prestonise and Dr. Mark Lusnar have been passionate users of the communication languages process for years and have encouraged me to develop simple communication tools to help people become radical communicators.

Also of incredible help have been: Ken Blanchard, who later shares his deep wisdom about adapting Servant Leadership to all relationships; Richard Blackaby, who helped me to write succinctly like a Taskmaster/Doer; Mike Freeman, who modeled a passionate Energizer's heart for change; Rob Jackson, an awesome Participator and servant listener; Vince Siciliano a powerful truth teller and Martha Lawrence, an insightful editor and priceless liaison. The Colonel helped me to write parts of this book to appeal to our readers who were Analyzers.

Of monumental importance to me in the writing of this book and in collaborating with Ken Blanchard has been Francisco Gomez. Francisco helped me to position radical listening as a required learning competency for servant leadership in both English and Spanish.

Thanks also to my men's group accountability partners for the past year to which I owe more than I can ever repay.

Neal St. Clair, Alan Casteran and Derek Thomas have been the trusted members of my tech support team, working behind the scenes to produce the online communication language technology referenced to in this book. I want to give extra special thanks to Sarah Funderburke and the team at Liberty University Press for their unparalleled support in getting this book from concept to paper in my lifetime.

My brother Tom Brunstetter and his wife Sabra, with Paradise Video and Film have been the driving force to produce a wide range of applications for radical servant listening that can be used on "hand-held" devices, as well as other media.

I want to thank my family including Sean, Teresa, Danise, Aaron and Michael for the listening lessons I have learned with and through them. Our youngest two daughters get timely kudos: Dana for being an insightful literary reviewer and Christen for being my model of persistence towards task completion.

I also want to thank my first mentor (Brother) Pat O'Brien for his mentorship while I was attending Bishop Armstrong/Christian Brothers High School in Sacramento, California. Pat taught me how to listen by doing it. Pat was also an encouraging "golf coach" and dear friend at a time when I needed one.

Most of all I want to thank my wife Carolyn for her love, support and patience throughout the seemingly lifelong transition that has been the fodder for this book.

CHAPTER 1
NO PAIN = NO GAIN

"Listening is a magnetic and strange thing, a creative force. The friends who listen to us are the ones we move toward. When we are listened to, it creates us, makes us unfold and expand."
— Karl Menninger [15]

HEARING IS NOT LISTENING

Thump Thump......Thump Thump........ Thump Thump. These are the first sounds each of us heard when in our mother's womb.   Medical scientists tell us that the ability to hear sound is the first human sense developed "in utero" i.e., in the womb, and that the first sound we hear is probably the beat of a heart. [16] Wow, what a way to begin our lives: listening to our mother's heart and then her voice before we even leave the womb. Is it any wonder that most of us were (and are) comforted more by our mother's voice than any other?

With such an awesome beginning why are most of us such extremely poor listeners? The answer is not all that complicated. Natural hearing is not the same as *learned listening*!

After decades of studying and teaching people how to communicate effectively I have come to the conclusion that most of us are *naturally poor listeners*. We don't know how to listen effectively because:

1) We mistakenly believe that "doing what comes naturally" is the only way to listen.
2) Most of us have learned how to listen from people who did not know how to listen themselves. We therefore are unaware that we don't know how to listen effectively.
3) When we finally realize we need to listen better we also discover that improving our listening will be embarrassing, humbling and painful. As a result we rationalize that our current listening is "good enough" and that we have more important things to worry about. Bottom line is that we talk-the-talk but most of us never walk-the-walk of improved listening behavior.

Let's be clear. Hearing is being aware of noise i.e., the natural stimulation we experience using our physical hearing equipment which then sends signals to our brain that we heard the noise. Listening, on the other hand, is our learned ability to transform that noise into something meaningful that benefits us and others! Voila! Here is the root of the generic listening problem. We may inherit the natural ability to hear sounds but our ability to "decode" these sounds and to communicate effectively needs to be taught and learned. (Some of us have issues with the physical hearing equipment, which complicates the listening process. Being hearing impaired is more challenging than I ever imagined.)

As the oldest of seven siblings, parent of seven kids and grandparent of 14 grandkids, I have learned firsthand that listening behavior is *caught not taught*. I "caught" my ability to listen largely by modeling my parents who were highly selective listeners at best. Until ten years ago I had developed lifelong habits of poor listening with no real clue as to how inadequate my actual listening had become. I for one can testify that the majority of my interpersonal failures including most of the pain I have experienced and inflicted on others can be attributed to my poor listening reinforced over time. All the new electronic gadgets popular in America today have made my listening worse, not better.

PERFECT PRACTICE MAKES PERFECT

Fred my golf coach had it right. He told me that to substantially change my game I had to do something radical with my swing. I had to endure the pain of changing my current bad golfing swing habits. What made changing my golf swing more complicated was that my flawed swing occasionally resulted in a good shot. More importantly I was comfortable with my poor swing. Fred helped me to understand "no pain=no gain," up close and personal. It was entirely up to me. I could opt for the half-hearted method and expect less dramatic improvement or go for the gusto and transform my golf game. In my life I have had so much natural ability I had a tendency to take the easy way out, i.e., avoid the pain and fake it until I made it.

My poor listening behaviors have been as powerful an example of opportunity wasted, as my golf game. I habitually avoided changes in various parts of my life that did not come quickly and that were not all that painful. I knew I should lose that extra weight by dieting and exercise. However, the anticipated pain associated with food denial and increased exercise is greater than the anticipated pleasure of being lighter so I talked-the-talk but didn't walk the walk. I desired the outcome but was not willing to change my poor dietary and exercising behavior. Like many, I made attempts to lose weight in January each year, but by March I was back to my usual lifestyle. You will be faced with the same dilemma after you finish this book. You can go low-key and get low-key results OR you can walk-the-talk of effective listening and complete the Call to Action with your inner circle and then with others.

In the twilight of my career I have become a passionate listening practitioner because I have seen firsthand the pain associated with poor listening and the untold joy that occurs when people learn to listen and communicate extremely well! I believe most people completely underestimate the negative effect poor listening behavior has on their experiences of love, intimacy, mutual respect, trust and growth. I suspect that unknowingly your listening may be limiting you more than you realize. Do yourself a favor! Take the listening assessment in chapter two and see how you fare as a servant listener. (For a 360° version of the Listening Assessment where others anonymously rate you in addition to self-rating please go to: www.itonlyhurtswhenilisten.com)

Improved listening is very much like losing weight. Both involve overcoming poor behavior ingrained over time. Both require a paradigm shift in our attitudes and beliefs so that sustained change can occur. Both require the mastery of personal pleasure and pain management. Both require the unlearning of bad behaviors and the learning of new and proficient replacement behaviors over time.

We will demonstrate in this book that radical servant listening is the firm foundation upon which all healthy human interaction is built. First we will get the causes and examples of poor listening out in the open. We will discover the ways we tend to naturally "fall short" as listeners. We will then discover a new listening paradigm and show you how to replace your dysfunctional listening behaviors with more functional ones. We will then supercharge your personal belief system with radical servant listening skills that have the potential to transform your life.

CHAPTER ONE: LESSONS LEARNED

- The ability to hear begins in the womb and first sounds are probably a mother's heart and later her voice
- *Hearing* and *Listening* are not as interchangeable as we think they are
- We are all "naturally poor listeners"
- Effective Listening is *Taught* not *Caught*
- Perfect Practice Makes Perfect
- Radical Servant Listening is Transformational
- As far as improving your listening goes… NO PAIN = NO GAIN

Before we begin your listening transformation let's establish a baseline for your current listening proficiency. Chapter two is a self-assessment of your listening effectiveness and how you think others would rate you on the same listening behaviors. You will have a chance to complete the ratings and use this self information in chapters 3-10 to gauge your proficiency in each area of measured listening proficiency.

CHAPTER 2
MY LISTENING ASSESSMENT

Please honestly rate yourself as a listener by answering the following questions. Resist the temptation to become a legend in your own mind or something that you are not. Your candor will help you identify both your listening strengths as well as areas on which you may need to work. Please rate how often you behave in the manner described for each item from 1-4. In addition, please do another rating, and this time put yourself in the shoes of those around you and do your best to rate how you think they perceive the frequency of your behaviors.

Therefore please make two ratings:

1) Self Column: SELF RATING
2) Others Column: How OTHERS would rate you

Please use the rating scale below and enter 1, 2, 3 or 4 in both columns for each item.

Rating Scale:
4 = Almost Always 3 = Most of the time 2 = Sometimes 1 = Seldom

	SELF	OTHERS
1) I show empathy and caring when listening to others	___	___
2) I listen with the desire to be influenced	___	___
3) I let others complete their thoughts and sentences before responding	___	___
4) I listen more than I speak when interacting with others	___	___
5) I listen without making quick judgments about what others are saying	___	___

6) When I am under extreme stress my listening behavior does not change ___ ___

7) I "get" the underlying meaning when others speak ___ ___

8) I encourage others to speak first when we are interacting ___ ___

9) I respond objectively and non-defensively when I completely disagree with others ___ ___

10) If I do get upset with others I am able to mask my true feelings well ___ ___

11) I focus fully on the person who is speaking with me at the time ___ ___

12) I listen to others with openness and trust despite any negative past history ___ ___

13) I plan ahead well to minimize stressful and/or emotional interactions ___ ___

14) I am good at putting myself in others' shoes as I listen to them ___ ___

15) I am as concerned with how people are feeling as I am about what they are saying ___ ___

16) I do well at focusing on context and circumstances when I listen to others ___ ___

17) I bite my tongue when required rather than responding impulsively ___ ___

18) I am able to give people reflective feedback as to what they said without "spin" ___ ___

19) I give people the benefit of the doubt when I don't fully understand ___ ___

20) I control my emotions with difficult people and under trying circumstances ___ ___

21) I flex well to the expectations of those speaking with me ___ ___

Totals ___ ___

Here is how to score and use your results from the Listening Assessment above:

1) Overall Listening Rating: Self and Other
   a. Add up your scores for the 21 items for both Self and Other
   b. Use the chart below to see where your scores compare to other ratees

2) Overall Listening Grade Ranges: (column totals)
   (A) 84-74: Exceptional
   (B) 73-58: Good
   (C) 57-50: Fair
   (D) 49-below: Poor

3) Individual Listening Grade Ranges: (average of the three items)
   (A) 4.0-3.50: Exceptional
   (B) 3.49-2.8: Good
   (C) 2.7-2.3: Fair
   (D) 2.2-below: Poor

HERE IS THE SCORING PROCESS FOR EACH OF THE NEXT 7 CHAPTERS:

1) Transpose the ratings from your Listening Assessment to the corresponding three questions at the beginning of Chapters 3-10.
2) Add up results for that area.
3) Score yourself on that area using the Individual Listening Grade Ranges.

THE PURPOSE OF THE SELF-LISTENING ASSESSMENT is to build your conscious awareness as to your listening strengths and weaknesses. This awareness should help you to focus on specific listening behaviors you need to replace and new behaviors you need to begin. During Relationship Transformation (chapter 16) you will have a chance to develop an action plan to transform your listening in every relationship in your life, present and future.

THE PURPOSE OF THE OTHER LISTENING ASSESSMENT is to help you become aware of the need to be skilled in your ability to put yourself in other people's shoes and spirit. One of the fundamental habits of a servant listener is the ability to understand and appreciate what is going on inside those around him/her. If you find the "other" exercise difficult I suspect you need to work on your "understanding others" behaviors more than you may realize.

THE PURPOSE FOR THE 360° FEEDBACK is to get anonymous feedback as to how others rate your listening behavior from their perspective. The average of your ratings tends to be more objective that your own self-assessment and will give you the wake-up call we promised. You must take the online version of the Listening Assessment to receive this 360° feedback.

Go to: www.itonlyhurtswhenilisten.com

CHAPTER 3
ME FIRST TO HUMBLE HEART

"People don't care how much you know until they know how much you care."
— Theodore Roosevelt [17]

HEART CONDITION	SELF	OTHERS
1) I show empathy and caring when listening to others	____	____
8) I encourage others to speak first when we are interacting	____	____
15) I am as concerned with how people are feeling as much as what they are saying	____	____
Averaged Totals	____	____
Grade	____	____

Rating Scale: 4 = Almost Always 3 = Most of the time 2 = Sometimes 1 = Seldom

Grade Ranges:
4.0-3.50: Exceptional 3.49-2.8: Good 2.7-2.3: Fair 2.2-below: Poor

We recognize pleasure as the first good innate in us, and from pleasure we begin every act of choice and avoidance, and to pleasure we return again, using the feeling as the standard by which we judge every good.
— Epicurus (342-270 BCE)

Epicurus highlights our natural tendency toward hedonism i.e., to seek pleasure and to avoid pain. This pleasure-seeking and pain-avoiding behavior is one of the most fundamental weaknesses in our listening behavior because it tilts the listening playing field. We can observe this seek pleasure/avoid pain phenomenon from newborn infants to elderly Alzheimer's patients. Our physical nature seeks to be comfortable and to enjoy whatever is pleasurable to us. This behavior is probably related in some way to our survival instincts. Pleasure is associated with enhancing and prolonging life. Pain is both a signal of imminent danger, and in some cases, signals our eventual mortality. As a result we tend to hear what we want to hear and ignore (avoid) what may be too painful to hear. The natural consequence of seeking pleasure/avoiding pain is that we become self-centered and myopic. Overcoming our natural pleasure/pain wiring requires systematic and sustained transformation that involves changing ineffective but comfortable behaviors and forming new ones to replace them that are not so comfortable at first. The pleasure-pain phenomenon plays a major role in how we listen from the "womb to the tomb."

POOR LISTENING TRAPS

My first wife and I were blessed with two children early in our marriage, and two more came fairly quickly after that. After my wife passed away I remarried and our current crew of seven is a combination of hers, mine and ours. At this writing we have 14 grandchildren, two daughters who have not married, and married kids who desire to have children. I share this with you because I realize now that like most well-intentioned parents we fell into the "poor listening" trap with all our kids. In our desire to nurture them to be healthy and self-sufficient we did what most parents do. Our parental goal was to have them grow up to become productive, self-sufficient and loving adults. Looking back we now realize that "Me," "My," "Mine" and later "I" were some of the first words they learned after "ma ma" and "da da!" We were so enthusiastic about teaching Sean (our first-born) and Teresa (who came a year later) to speak. Each new word from their mouths was greeted with cheers, claps and vocal celebrations. I realize now that we never deliberately taught Sean and Teresa how to listen. In retrospect, we modeled how to listen (poorly) and they quickly mimicked us. I realize now that listening is *caught* not taught.

Medical scientists confirm that humans come into the world the most helpless of all species and at maturity they become the most self-sufficient. Sean and Teresa's complete dependency on us to survive infancy combined well with our parental preoccupation with teaching them self-expression and self-sufficiency. We never taught them the value of "selfless" listening. Based upon anecdotal information from thousands of parents with whom I have worked with over the years, poor parental listening is more the norm than the exception. Parents can get away with poor listening with their kids until puberty and that is when the failure to communicate hits the dysfunctional fan in most families. Why? I believe that all families (and teams for that matter) are dysfunctional and the root cause is that they are naturally poor listeners.

I also suggest that most teachers at all levels don't teach students how to listen either. They too are modeling a natural listening style that is highly selective and speaker-driven. Don't get me wrong. Teachers *do* reward students who listen well and punish those who don't. They just don't teach students listening skills. Sports coaches don't teach youth how to listen either, only how to play the sport. They too reward kids who listen *and* perform well. Supervisors don't teach employees how to listen. Like teachers and sports coaches, supervisors tend to reward people who listen well, and punish those who don't. Of course, there are exceptions where parents, teachers, coaches and supervisors take a personal interest in someone and exhibit exceptional listening skills. Exceptional listening by an adult figure in a child's life is the exception not the rule. We need a better communications model than the speech driven and highly selective listening behavior of parents, teachers, coaches and supervisors.

LISTENING BY FIRST WALKING AROUND

My life-long passion has been to help others communicate well. I picked up the communication baton from my father Doc Brunstetter who was one of the first industrial psychologists working directly for the president (and not human resources). Doc moved his office from his comfortable ivory tower at the City College of New York (CCNY) to the shop floor at Republic Aviation in Long Island, New York. Doc was a pioneer who said being close to the people that produced the F-85 fighter planes was a defining moment in his career. Doc told me he learned more listening to people in the cafeteria on the third shift than all the collective time he ever spent in any board room at Republic. Doc was a wise man who listened extremely well when he was with people at work. He impressed on me early in my career that if I wanted to be effective trainer/facilitator in the workplace I needed to go out and understand trainees in their world. I needed to understand and speak their language, feel their pain and share in their joys. That's why he put his office on the shop floor. He was doing "leading by walking around" long before Tom Peters made it fashionable. Doc showed me the value of *listening by walking around.*

Doc's passion for learning "shop talk" (different from talking shop) rubbed off on me early in my career in Industrial Relations and later in my Ph.D. dissertation. I am a toolmaker who wants to provide handles for people to grab and communicate better with. Doc showed me how to listen at work and only recently have I put into practice what he so wisely taught me years ago. Now that I am a re-born listener, so to speak, I have labored long and hard to develop a systematic approach to communication effectiveness that would transform relationships in my life and now in the lives of others.

ADULT LISTENING

Malcolm Knowles, Ph.D. was my Ph.D. mentor/adviser and I was blessed to have this reputed "Father of Adult Learning" as my academic adviser and coach. Malcolm came from a humanistic orientation where self-actualization was the prime objective of adult learning. He believed that the mission of educators was to assist adult learners in realizing their full emotional, psychological, and intellectual potential. Learning how adults listen differently than children listen was a key component of his self-actualization model. He shared with me his four assumptions about adults as learners:

(1) Adults tend to be more self-directed as a result of their maturity,
(2) Adults possess personal histories (schema) which define their identity and serve as a resource for experiential learning,
(3) Motivation in adults is directed to more personally and socially relevant learning,
(4) Adult learners are interested in immediate problem-solving.

The overlap between the adult learner and servant listener is significant in my view. Both are focused exclusively on the needs of those being served. Both involve the impact of prior learning and experience on present behavior. Both suggest the profound implications of perspective on learning in general and listening in particular. Finally both require that we clearly understand and speak the language of those being served if we are to listen and learn effectively.

A BETTER LISTENING MOUSETRAP WITH A HEART

The Radical Listening model can be taught as well as caught. After extensive study, trial and error, training and experimenting we are now ready to share our learning with you. We have identified the most critical listening flaws and the most effective replacement behaviors. You don't need to walk on water to become an exceptional listener; you just need to know where the rocks are. You do not need to experience as much pain learning to listen as in the past. Our hope is that you will be able to identify and discard your poor listening behaviors. You will then be able to transform every relationship in your life using the new listening skills you acquire. Here are some powerful examples of humble servant listeners.

Vic was a gentle Italian with dark brown eyes and sincere charm. He was a guy who everyone liked and wanted to be with. In the three years we worked together I learned more from him about life, people and the real world of "work" than any other person in my life before or since. Vic did many things well but what he did best was listen.

He made time for me and when I spoke with him he treated me as if I was the most important person in his world. He seemed to hang on my every word and wanted to hear more. When he did speak it was always from his heart. I knew that he cared about me and I learned to pour out my innermost thoughts and feelings to him. He never judged or chastised me about my feelings. He would always conclude by asking me "How can I help?" Vic was a person that took the time to listen to me when most others wouldn't give me a thought. He was there for me when I was down and out and hurting. He had an incredible ability to listen despite the circumstances. The best part about Vic is that he truly cared about me and understood me…without strings.

Vic was my first supervisor-friend and I will never forget his stewardship in our relationship. As I matured he challenged me more but always in a way that built me up and encouraged me. He died of cancer years later but his legacy lives on in people like me. Vic touched others with his humble heart and his helpful spirit. Vic is a prime example of a humble servant listener.

* * *

Helen Keller was a different kind of servant listener who served millions of people through effort, passion, persistence and love. Keller became deaf and blind shortly after her birth on June 27, 1880, and yet she played a leading role in one of the most of the significant political, social, and cultural movements of the 20th century. Throughout her lifetime (1880-1968) she worked unceasingly to improve the lives of people with disabilities, and she never heard a word and never saw a face. Not coincidentally Helen Keller had a "heart condition" for people and was a servant listener even though she could not hear or see. She used her big heart and her ability to touch, smell and taste to compensate for her inability to see or hear.

* * *

My final example of radical servant listening is Agnes Bojaxhiu who was born on August 27, 1910, in Skopje, Macedonia. In 1948 Agnes came across a dying woman in the streets of Calcutta and cared for her until the woman died in her arms. For the next 50 years Agnes learned to communicate with and understand the poor where they lived …in the gutters of Calcutta. Agnes had two "heart conditions:" One was a loving heart for the poor and downtrodden and the other was a heart weakened over time by years of strenuous physical, emotional and spiritual work. Though frail and bent, with numerous ailments, Agnes always returned to her work with the abject poor who received her compassionate care until she died on September 5, 1997.

Agnes, better known as Mother Teresa, had a humble heart that allowed her to listen to and understand others so poor that they could never repay her for her gifts of service. She literally walked in others shoes, slept where they slept, ate what they ate and smelled what they smelled. Mother Teresa is a prime example of humble servant leadership and servant listening who did more than walk in others' shoes. She shared their language, their culture, their joys but mostly their pain. She was able to transform people because she understood them and because she cared about them and they knew it. Her efforts affected billions of people.

I am not suggesting that to become a radical listener we need to live in the streets of Calcutta or that we must work with the deaf and dumb to make a difference in people's lives. Some of us may want to become that radical in our service of others, but we can make a difference right now with those with whom we interact every day.

What I am suggesting, however, is that we need to have Teresa's heart, humility and passion for listening if we want to make a difference in others' lives. We need to use all our senses as we experience others' joy and pain, just as Helen Keller did. Finally, we need to make the time for others when they need us, to listen to them as if they were the most important person in our life, like Vic did for me. We need to start listening with a heart condition to those closest to us, and eventually develop a caring heart for everyone else without strings.

A SHORT HISTORY OF SERVANT LISTENING

I have been intrigued for years by the concept of the "servant leader" because of its radical call for the leader to transition from self-serving to serving others. I first heard the term "servant leader" in a seminar and later book by Ken Blanchard. Since then, I have come across many references to servant leadership by Ken and other noted leadership gurus, such as Robert Greenleaf, John Maxwell, Stephen Covey, and Larry Spears.

Apparently the phrase servant leader was first used by Robert K. Greenleaf in an essay entitle *The Servant as Leader*.[18] He writes:

> *"The servant leader is SERVANT first. That person is sharply different from one who is LEADER first."*

Ken Blanchard describes the servant leader as deeply committed to understanding and helping others to achieve their goals. Further he describes the power of listening as the start point for servant leadership.

> *"The servant leader feels that once the direction is clear his or her role is to help those being led to achieve their goals. The servant leader seeks to help people win through teaching and coaching individuals so that they can do their best. You need to listen to your people, praise them, support them and redirect them when they deviate from their goals."*[19]

Blanchard also emphasizes the servant leader's transformation from selfish to selfless in the way he/she listens to others, helps them and then focuses the credit on them as well.

> *"Servant leadership is easy for people with high self-esteem. Such people have no problem giving credit to others and have no problem listening to other people for ideas. They have no problem in building other people up and they don't feel other people's success threatens them in any way."*[20]

In his *Ten Principles of Servant Leadership* Larry Spears lays the foundation for all servant leadership by describing servant listening.

> *Traditionally, leaders have been valued for their communication and decision making skills. Servant-leaders must reinforce these important skills by making a deep commitment to listening intently to others. Servant-leaders seek to identify and clarify the will of a group. They seek to listen receptively to what is being said (and not said). Listening also encompasses getting in touch with one's inner voice, and seeking to understand what one's body, spirit, and mind are communicating.*[21]

In order to become an effective servant listener we need to listen with all
our senses, as Helen Keller taught us. We also need to develop a Mother Teresa-
like heart for people. From all that I have read about Mother Teresa she was
an incredibly empathetic listener.

*"It's not how much we do, but how much love we put into the doing. It's is not
how much we give, but how much love we put into the giving."*
— Mother Teresa [22]

THE "ME FIRST" PROBLEM

We don't listen well because we don't know how to. How we listen
was "caught" from our parents, teachers and coaches early in our lives and
employers later, not many of whom were trained to be effective listeners
or teachers of effective listening. This collective and well-intentioned
overemphasis on self-expression has helped us to become self-sufficient but
not very good at listening. Grounded in hedonism and narcissism, we have
learned to listen from a "Me First" perspective. Ironically the very skills
that make us self-determined and self-sufficient tend to block our ability to
become highly functional as a servant listener.

"None are so blind as those who choose not to listen."
— P. John Brunstetter

THE RADICAL "HEART CONDITIONING" SOLUTION

In order to become an effective servant listener we need to practice the
following listening behaviors.

1. **Let Others Speak First Whenever and Wherever Possible.**
   This is a simple yet humbling paradigm shift for most of us. Letting
   others go first in the speaking processes is a starter. There is a plethora
   of other opportunities to wait until others have gone first. Driving,
   grocery checkout, ticket lines, buffets, etc... are just some of the
   humbling opportunities to let others go first. Routinely encouraging
   others to speak is truly *radical*.

2. **Stop ALL Self-Promotion and Start Promoting Others.** Wow,
   this is a tough one for some of us. As we sincerely focus our positive

energy on the others (not glad handing) we build others up and in a very real way we show people that we truly care about them with a servant's humble heart. Be careful not to overdo your promotion of family members and subordinates because indirectly you may be seen as promoting yourself. Radically promote others and let them promote you *if* and *when* they desire.

3. **Serve the Needy UP CLOSE AND PERSONAL.** I believe that changing our listening paradigm is best served by helping others who are less fortunate. In addition to your financial support, the poor and downtrodden need your time and your "hands on" service.

a. Work for a Homeless Shelter, Crises Prevention Center, Soup Kitchen, Food Bank or similar organization where you get to rub elbows and share your lives with the poor and needy. You will be amazed how your heart for people is softened after you "serve" them.

b. Sign up for Habitat for Humanity and help build homes for people in need in your local community. Just show up and they will use whatever you have.

c. Volunteer at your local church, scout troop or community to serve as people did after Hurricane Katrina or the earthquake in Japan.

d. Serve those caring for men and women transitioning from prison, such as Restoration House in Monroe, NC. As you serve others, listen to them with a humble and compassionate heart. You don't need to impress poor people. You just need to serve them and listen to them. You don't necessarily need to win them over by giving them money per se. Give them the gift of a listening and loving you! After experiencing the poor and disadvantaged up-close-and-personal you will change the way you listen and the way you communicate.

The radical calling I suggest is that you practice these **all** the time and with **all** relationships and **all** interactions not just when you "feel like it" or when you are in a "listening mood" or when you are with trusted friends and comfortable family.

RELATED RADICAL LISTENERS' PLEDGE
I will ask others to speak first as often as possible.

CHAPTER THREE: LESSONS LEARNED

- Our natural inclination toward hedonism leads invariably to a "Me First" worldview
- Children are taught to *verbalize* and not necessarily to listen
- Adults listen naturally with an intention to be self-directed and self-sufficient
- "Others go First" behavior is unnatural but it also shows how much we really care
- Promoting others rather than ourselves requires humility and sincerity
- Replace bad listening with servant listening
- "Heart conditioning" is a change in both your behavior and attitude from self-service to serving others
- Serve the poor and needy with your time as well as your money
- Learn to listen with all your senses as Helen Keller did
- Develop a Mother Teresa "humble heart condition" especially for people in need
- When you are interacting with others make them feel like they are the most important person in the world

CHAPTER 4
COMMON SENSE TO DISCERNMENT

"We don't see things as they are; we see them as we are."
— *Anaïs Nin* [23]

DISCERNMENT		SELF	OTHERS
2) I listen with the desire to be influenced		⎯⎯	⎯⎯
9) I do not respond defensively when I completely disagree with others		⎯⎯	⎯⎯
16) I do well at focusing on context and circumstances when I listen to others		⎯⎯	⎯⎯
Averaged Totals		⎯⎯	⎯⎯
Grade		⎯⎯	⎯⎯

Rating Scale: 4 = Almost Always 3 = Most of the time 2 = Sometimes 1 = Seldom

Grade Ranges:
4.0-3.50: Exceptional 3.49-2.8: Good 2.7-2.3: Fair 2.2-below: Poor

Being *completely honest*... How would you react to each of the following circumstances if no one was watching you?

1. You go out in a torrential downpour to get something at the drug store and the only open space in the parking lot is right by the front door but it has a car parked covering two stalls. Being brutally honest, how would most people respond? How would you probably react and feel if no one was watching you?

2. You agree to meet a co-worker early for breakfast even though you are not a "morning person." You are hesitant because this person

historically has no sense of time and is habitually late but you agree anyway. Being brutally honest, what are your initial reactions and feelings when this person stands you up without letting you know?

3. You are driving home late at night and someone cuts right in front of you, forcing you to slam on your breaks and swerve onto the shoulder of the road to avoid a collision. As you catch your breath and your heart goes back into your chest, being brutally honest, how would most people react/feel? How would you react/feel if no one was watching?

Now, consider the following additional data & see if your perspective changes:

1. You get inside the drug store and see an elderly man lying on the floor breathing heavily. You overhear the druggist say "good thing this man was near the drug store when his nitroglycerin ran out." When you realize that this man was driving the car in the two stalls how would you react and how do you now feel? What has changed?

2. After you have breakfast alone, you get back to your office and try to use your cell phone and discover that your cell battery is dead. You put on a quick charge and listen to your messages. There is a message from the previous evening alerting you that a family member of the person you were to meet is ill and he wants to reschedule the meeting. Now what are your reactions and feelings? You still got up needlessly. What has changed?

3. You get your car back on the road and immediately pull into a gas station to get yourself together. When you look in the reflected glass you realize that you have been driving with your lights off. Now what are your reactions and feelings? The circumstances of being cut off have not changed. What has changed?

Here is another before/after scenario from Anaïs Nin that will tug on your heart strings:

A father got on the train with his four young children. He sat down quietly. His children proceeded to run amok up and down the aisles making quite a racket. A woman approached the father and said, "Why can't you do a better job of managing your children?" "I am sorry," he replied, "We just came from the hospital. You see we just survived a car accident that killed their mother."

The Anaïs Nin quote above captures the essence of these "before and after scenarios" quite well. We see things as *we are* at the time not as *they are*. Our perception is based on our own unique reality and we don't know what we don't know. As it pertains to listening to others the saying should go "We don't know what they know." When we understand other's perspectives and/ or have additional data, our impressions can change dramatically. In all four cases, initial emotions were trumped later by a new and more complete perspective.

THE LOST COIN

Jack was a poor craftsman who had just lost a rare coin his dad had given him just before he died. He immediately went out after dark and started to grovel on his hands and knees underneath a streetlight searching desperately for his lost coin. One of Jack's friends asked him if he knew where he had lost the coin and Jack said "No not really." His friend then said, "Why then are you searching underneath that particular street light." Jack replied, "Because the light is the brightest here."

We tend to respond to events and challenges more like Jack than we may think. We see things around us based on where our light is the brightest. We base our assessments on our own common sense i.e., we assume that our perspective is the only reality because the light is the brightest there. Another way to understand how we listen selectively is to consider the following saying, "If the only tool you have is a hammer, all your problems are nails."

THE FOUR BLIND MEN FABLE [24]

Four blind men came across an elephant one day. Each one of them encountered a different part of the animal: one the trunk, one a leg, one an ear and one the tail. Upon inspecting the animal from their individual vantage points, each came to a very different perception of the animal they were touching:

"Wow! What a large and powerful snake," said blind man #1 with his hands on the trunk.

"Not So! It's a tree not a snake," retorted blind man #2 with his hands on the leg.

"You are both wrong. It's obviously a bird with big wings," chimed blind man #3 with his hands on the ear.

"I don't have a clue how you all arrived at your conclusions! This animal is most assuredly a lion and I suggest we move along quickly," snapped blind man #4 who was holding the wagging tail.

OUR BRAIN USES SCHEMAS TO CODE EXPERIENCE

We interpret the elephants around us like the blind men in the fable. Much of our perception is based on our genetics and limited prior experiences. In my Ph.D. research I discovered that we all "encode" and categorize experiences and place them in "schema" which is then stored in "buckets" in our brain. There are hundreds of thousands of schema and combinations in our brain but they tend to be sorted first by what we perceive is pleasurable and then what is painful. There are schemas to accommodate any circumstance. Our schemas are the "libraries" that our brain goes to for the information that feeds our "common sense." What we call common sense is really not so common at all. Our decision making is based on highly selective bits and bytes stored in our brain. Like the blind men we make decisions based on the part of the elephant we are most familiar with and where the light is shining the brightest.

VISUAL (MIS)PERCEPTION

In the picture on the following page there are a variety of images that our brain can identify if we look close enough. First impressions are not the only impressions. Are the lines straight?

Similarly, what images do you see in the second picture?

THE COMMON SENSE PROBLEM

Common sense, the collective combination of all our sensory input, is both a blessing and a curse. The car in the two stalls, Jack's street light, the visual illusions and the elephant fable all bear an eerie likeness to how highly selective we are as perceivers and listeners. We are first of all, blind to most

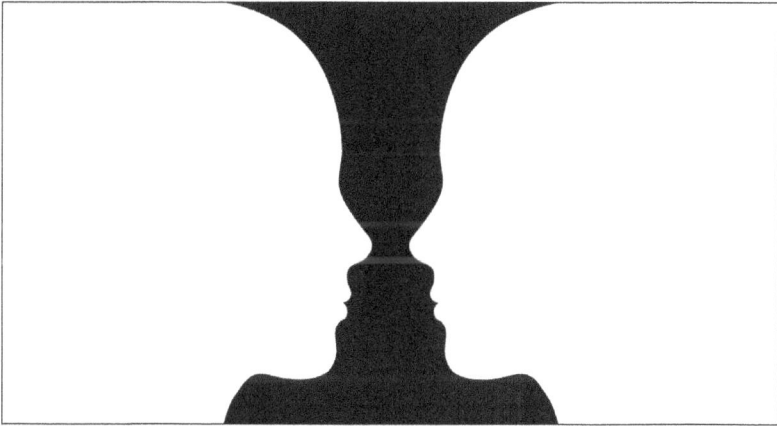

of what is being presented to us because it is dark in that area. We then give meaning to what we are hearing based on our limited experience, where our light is shining and what our not so common sense is telling us. Our nature also encourages us to act independently and to be self-serving. Seldom do we take the time to inspect "the elephant" from every angle and listen to others in order to get a more objective impression. Seldom do we look closer to discern the underlying message in a different light. Seldom do we look at things from others' unique perspective. Our common sense is not all that common and often not all that sensible.

THE RADICAL DISCERNMENT SOLUTION

Discernment is the unnatural answer to our natural tendency to use our common sense. When we are discerning we give ourselves a more clear and objective reality upon which to make decisions. Our nature and experience want us to believe that what we see is reality or it tells us "If it feels good do it!" As we learned earlier, what we see is not necessarily accurate or complete because all our perception goes through our own "dirty filters." Just because it "feels right or good" at the time does not mean it is the best thing to do. The result: Our perception often becomes our enemy as well as our reality. Here are some radical servant listening behaviors to help you overcome your natural perceptual limitations:

1. **Wait at least 24 Hours** before you make any critical decision. This gives you time to calmly consider your choices and the implications of those choices. Looking at something the next day also gives you a different perspective.
2. **Listen with the Desire to be Influenced,** which is more than keeping an open mind. The radical servant listener is passionate about wanting to learn and grow, and it shows.
3. **Identify "Truth Tellers"** around you and periodically share your perspectives and concerns before key decision making. Periodically ask for and receive brutally honest feedback and then listen intently without being defensive.
4. **Empower an "Accountability Partner"** to hold you accountable for saying what you mean and meaning what you say so you avoid becoming a "legend in your own mind." Spouses are not completely objective accountability partners so identify a non-relative, preferably of the same sex, who can be completely open, honest and supportive.

"If silence is golden then unnecessary speaking is fool's gold"
— *P. John Brunstetter, Ph.D.*

RELATED RADICAL LISTENERS' PLEDGE
I will keep my mouth shut and my ears, mind and heart wide open.

CHAPTER FOUR: LESSONS LEARNED

- All listening is selective and based on what genetics and experience have been stored in our brain
- Initially, we listen by coding and sorting experiences into "pay attention" or "ignore" categories
- Listening is a function of all the senses especially hearing and vision
- Our natural senses combine to create "common sense" (which is not necessarily common and not necessarily sensible)
- Common sense is both functional and deceptive at times
- By nature, we tend to hear what we want to hear and see what we want to see
- Discernment is the unnatural approach to perceiving, decision making and action
- Develop the habit of waiting before making important decisions
- Listen with the radical intention of being influenced
- Bring "truth tellers" around you to help you see what you can't or don't want to see
- Engage an objective "accountability partner" to help you become more wise in decisions and actions

ME NOW TO MATURITY

"Instant gratification takes too long."
— *Carrie Fisher* [25]

MATURITY   SELF   OTHERS

3) I listen patiently and let people complete
    their thoughts before responding   ____   ____
10) I respond objectively and non defensively
    when I completely disagree with others   ____   ____
17) I bite my tongue when required rather than
    responding impulsively   ____   ____

    Averaged Totals   ____   ____
    Grade   ____   ____

Rating Scale: 4 = Almost Always 3 = Most of the time 2 = Sometimes 1 = Seldom

Grade Ranges:
4.0-3.50: Exceptional 3.49-2.8: Good 2.7-2.3 Fair 2.2-below: Poor

DELAYED GRATIFICATION

Young children find it more difficult to delay gratification than older children. When kindergartners in one study were offered a choice between getting a small candy bar immediately or a larger one later, 72 percent chose the smaller candy bar. This number decreased to 67 percent among first and second graders and 49 percent for third and fourth graders. By the fifth and sixth grades it had fallen to 38 percent, nearly half the rate for kindergartners.

One of the by-products of our hedonistic nature is an insatiable natural desire for immediate gratification. We are wired for impatience by nature and early life conditioning. Immediate gratification is childish behavior that says "I want what I want and I want it NOW!"

We all have been exposed to the pain of delayed gratification whether deciding to avoid dessert in order to lose a few pounds; giving up smoking in order to live a longer and more pleasant life or a host of circumstances where we have to postpone pleasure and often experience short term pain. The skill of delayed gratification is a *prerequisite* to radical servant listening.

When it comes to listening many of us are in the first grade and want to eat our smaller candy bar *now* rather than listen to someone else and get a bigger candy bar later.

THE "ME NOW" PROBLEM

We are conditioned to seek pleasure, avoid pain, and to do so quickly. We therefore tend to have knee-jerk reactions when someone is speaking to us. Knee-jerk reactions are doubly dangerous because they trigger a slew of raw and unfiltered thoughts stored in schema in our "preconscious." Our natural and immature self wants to *release* these raw feelings and beliefs without being filtered by values, discernment, reason and/or time. Many times, hormonal activities can also trigger our quick verbal responses especially when we do not agree with something spoken. Within milliseconds of hormonal release into our blood stream, the raw words in our preconscious race unflatteringly to our lips.

At times we have all felt "Why am I saying this?" or "Why am I going here?" or worse yet "Why on earth did I say that?" after our serotonin, adrenaline and other hormones have triggered us to empty our preconscious mind on others. When we speak quickly without discernment we create unnecessary communication hurdles, pain and the need for damage control. We are naturally wired to act like a microwave oven instead of a crock-pot when it comes to listening. A habit of quick response makes servant listening virtually impossible.

THE RADICAL MATURITY SOLUTION

My definition of maturity is: **The ability to consciously delay immediate gratification and to wait patiently for a more desirable alternative.**

It takes commitment, discipline and perfect practice to overcome our natural impatience when it comes to listening. Our natural self-orientation pressures us to focus on the short-term and the result is we block out our learned ability to listen well. The longer our response time, the quicker our hormones can return to normal. Discernment needs physical, emotional and temporal space to operate effectively.

The combination of "Me First" and "Me Now" are a dynamic duo that require root canal surgery before replacement behavior can begin. Here are some ways to mature as a radical listener:

1. **Self-Denial:**
   a. Periodically abstain from food, drink and/or other gratifications. You need to learn how to control your appetites or they will control you. The health benefits to mature self-denial can be significantly positive.
   b. Go on a speaking diet. Work hard to say less and mean more. Be concise in your use of words by learning to use and need fewer words to explain yourself.

2. **Pause Before Responding:**
   a. Break the habit of immediately responding when someone speaks to you even if they ask you a question.
   b. Take a short breath and make sure you understand before responding.
   c. Reflect on what you think you heard before you open your mouth.
   d. Briefly rehearse key sound bites you heard in your head.

3. **Respond with a KISS (Keep it Short and Simple):**
   a. After you have paused then summarize what you thought the other person said in as few words as possible.
   b. Verify you heard what the speaker had intended to say.
   c. Recalibrate as required to get to clarity before you state your perspective.
   d. Then share your thoughts and how they compare/contrast to the speakers.

"Make a habit of dominating the listening and let the customer dominate the talking."
— Brian Tracy [26]

CHAPTER FIVE: LESSONS LEARNED

- We are naturally impatient listeners, listening like micro-waves not crockpots
- Our largely uninhibited preconscious mind drives us to respond quickly
- The faster we respond the less the quality control or truth checking
- Quick responses often send unintentional mixed signals
- Our natural instincts tend to push for immediate gratification and poor listening is the result
- Discernment is the solution to overcoming immediate gratification
- Self-denial helps us control our natural impatience
- Pausing before responding creates time and space for discernment to operate
- Reflecting what we heard focuses on clarity, not conflict

CHAPTER 6
VERBAL PROCESSING TO ACTIVE LISTENING

"Listen. Do not have an opinion while you listen because frankly, your opinion doesn't hold much water outside of your universe. Just listen. Listen until their brain has been twisted like a dripping towel and what they have to say is all over the floor."
— *Hugh Elliott* [27]

ACTIVE LISTENING   SELF   OTHERS

4) I listen more than I speak when interacting
with others   ____   ____
11) I focus fully on the person who is speaking
with me at the time   ____   ____
18) I am able to give people reflective feedback as to what they said without "spin"   ____   ____

Averaged Totals   ____   ____
Grade   ____   ____

Rating Scale: 4 = Almost Always 3 = Most of the time 2 = Sometimes 1 = Seldom

Grade Ranges:
4.0-3.50: Exceptional 3.49-2.8: Good 2.7-2.3 Fair 2.2-below: Poor

---

When two people get together there is a finite amount of time available to speak. Speaking time can be used in various ways. One party may speak, both may speak simultaneously or both can be silent together. We call this "airtime."

My mom, June, was an incredible mother, wife, grandmother, teacher and friend. Along with her long list of virtues was a small list of shortcomings. At the top of the latter list was her incessant need to talk and talk and talk. She was a classic airtime hog. She had a penetrating fear of silence that drove her to use every possible minute of airtime she could. I believe I have inherited my mom's penchant for talking too much. I now realize how much my over-talking has negatively affected many of my past and present relationships.

Nothing communicates sincere caring more than the amount of time we encourage others to speak and how we respond when then do. Of course the right balance of speaking and listening can change based on the environment, trust and the issues being discussed. The main point I want to make here is that our natural need to share our perspective tends to be more powerful than our unnatural desire to hear someone else's thoughts. From birth we have been conditioned and rewarded for speaking first. Changing lifelong behaviors is a challenge. When two people get together, each alternates from being a sender to being a receiver. When one party wants to be the sender most (if not all) times we call them an "air time hog." When we don't do what it takes to allow others to speak they become bored, disconnected and sometimes resentful.

THE VERBAL PROCESSING PROBLEM

When it comes to listening "nature abhors a vacuum." Silence gaps when interacting with others make most of us nervous and as a result we often speak to break the discomfort of silence. Often what we say during those times is not at all important because we are just filling in the uncomfortable space with words. Sometimes what we say is from our preconscious, and therefore can be problematic and potentially harmful. When others pause it is not necessarily an invitation for us to speak. They may be gathering their thoughts and/or trying to come up with the right way to say something. If we jump in we may knock them off track. When we speak we need to be careful not to do "verbal processing." Instead of thinking through what we want to say and how best to say it we begin verbalizing what we are thinking in our attempt to organize our thoughts. When we verbally process we frustrate others who don't understand that we are just babbling out loud trying to figure things out by hearing how the ideas sound. The habitual use of verbal processing and babble breaks down communication and trust.

THE RADICAL LISTENING SOLUTION

The servant listener takes the initiative to do what he/she can to create the appropriate balance between who is speaking and who is listening. Most of the time the best approach is to encourage others to speak first and then to listen actively when they do. As the issues unfold the servant listener is able to discern when and how much to speak. Here are some ways to balance the available airtime appropriately and effectively:

1. **Master your Fear of Silence.** Resist the urge to speak and let others have the floor especially at the beginning of verbal interactions. Create opportunity space for others to enter and share before you get your two cents worth. When you are speaking you miss the opportunity to learn more about others and what they are focused on.

2. **Create a Positive Communication Vacuum** or "safe opportunity space" by listening to others with sincere attention, focus and positive body language and your mouth shut. It's not just how much time we give others to speak but how we behave when they do. We can unintentionally (or intentionally) shut people out when we hog airtime.

3. **Encourage Others to Share** by asking questions, looking at your speaker and giving reflective feedback when appropriate. The natural danger here is that when others begin speaking we want to "help" them so we interrupt instead of actively listening.

4. **Make Sure Others are Ready to Hear What you Have to Say.** Until you convey that you understand someone else's perspective to their satisfaction you have not earned the right for them to listen intently to what you have to say on that subject.

"Many attempts to communicate are nullified by saying too much."
— *Robert Greenleaf* [28]

CHAPTER SIX: LESSONS LEARNED

- Airtime is the available time for someone to speak when two or more people are dialoguing
- Nature abhors a vacuum where listening is concerned, so people often just babble to break the uncomfortable silence; Others remain "frozen" and don't contribute when they ought to
- When we are speaking we are not listening very well. When we are not listening we are not learning. The more airtime we take the less we listen and therefor the less we learn
- The repeated abuse of airtime erodes relationships and trust
- Learn to use silence without fear
- Encourage others to explain their ideas and listen patiently when they do
- Actively attend to people when they are speaking to you
- Share your ideas after you have earned the right to do so
- Gauge others' readiness to hear what you have to say and speak accordingly

CHAPTER 7
JUDGMENT TO TRUST

"When you hold resentment toward another, you are bound to that person or condition by an emotional link that is stronger than steel. Forgiveness is the only way to dissolve that link and get free."
— *Catherine Ponder* [29]

TRUST	SELF	OTHERS
5) I listen without making quick judgments about what others are saying	____	____
12) I listen to others with openness and trust despite any negative past history	____	____
19) I give people the benefit of the doubt when I don't fully understand	____	____
Averaged Totals	____	____
Grade	____	____

Rating Scale: 4 = Almost Always 3 = Most of the time 2 = Sometimes 1 = Seldom

Grade Ranges:
4.0-3.50: Exceptional 3.49-2.8: Good 2.7-2.3 Fair 2.2-below: Poor

JUDGMENT AND PREJUDICE

One of the most dysfunctional listening behaviors is our natural tendency to be quick to judge others and their ideas. As demonstrated earlier we are all a unique combination of genetics and experiences percolating over time. We have developed core beliefs, attitudes and opinions about what is right and wrong based on our unique history. We all have biases and prejudices and "hot buttons" waiting to be pressed. Whenever someone starts speaking we quickly start comparing what we think they are saying to what we believe is the true or correct perspective. In essence we don't trust others' judgment as much as our own so we pre-judge them. The word prejudice comes from the Latin "prae" (pre) and "judicium" (judge).

Some psychologists believe that when we judge and later criticize others we are reacting to our own insecurities and possible failures in that subject area. There is a quote from Shakespeare that fits here "The lady doth protest too much, methinks."[30] Inadvertently we often signal a failing of our own when we start protesting too much.

As soon as there is the slightest disconnect with what we believe to be true we tend to stop listening fully and begin rehearsing our defensive reaction. Seldom do we give others the benefit of the doubt unless they have previously earned our trust. Instead of listening fully with an open mind and heart we default to distrusting and judgmental behavior. We initiate body language to signal our disagreement and sooner or later we jump in to express our disagreement verbally. Judgmental listening quickly breaks down the healthy communication process as all participants default to negative, defensive, distrusting and judgmental behavior.

THE JUDGMENT PROBLEM

Sometimes we describe our judgmental questioning as being a devil's advocate in the self-righteous belief that it is our responsibility to get out what we believe is the truth. Whether we interrupt the speaker or not our judgmental behavior sends negative signals to the speaker before he/she has had a chance to fully share what is on their mind. Prejudgment signals disrespect and a "holier than thou" attitude. Many times we prejudge because we have been hurt, wronged or in some way damaged by this person or someone else in our past. Lingering unforgiveness tends to impair our ability to listen objectively and with empathy. When we prejudge for any reason we stop being open to what others are saying and signal that our mind is closed and we are not interested in their perspective. When others perceive we are prejudging them they shut down communication and become defensive.

THE RADICAL TRUST AND FORGIVENESS SOLUTION

Overcoming prejudices and tendencies to prejudge begins with some spadework in the area of forgiveness. Even if you do not believe you have any issues with forgiveness you may discover some hidden issues that have been limiting your ability to become a servant listener if you dig a bit. You will not be able to trust anyone fully unless you let go of unforgiveness and vice versa. Here are some healthy steps to explore forgiveness and trust building in your life:

1. **Completely Forgive ALL those who have hurt you.** Wow, this is *radical*. Make an exhaustive list of all those who have damaged you. Check the ones that you have not *completely* forgiven. Holding on to even the slightest unforgiveness will weaken your heart condition for listening and inhibit your communication effectiveness. This is a tall order and may be extremely difficult especially if those you have not forgiven are deceased. Put self-forgiveness at the top of the list.
    a. Completely forgive everyone you have checked off.
    b. Burn the list and let it go!
    c. If you have a chance to interact with people on the list use your new listening habits to show that you really care about them and that you really trust them. Sharing your forgiveness with others directly is an option but you do run the risk of opening up old wounds or creating new ones. It may either be radical or foolish. You need to make that call carefully.

2. **Ask for Forgiveness from those you have hurt.** Make a second list of those you have hurt in your life, living or not.
    a. Then write a letter to each of them apologizing from your heart for your previous behavior and asking them for forgiveness
    b. Burn the letters. You don't need to talk about it again unless a specific situation requires you to do so. Again, sending the letters runs the risk of opening up old wounds and Pandora's Box. If you do send the letters be prepared to work through all the unresolved issues with this person or you will hurt them all the more.
    c. If you have ongoing contact with a person on your list use your new listening behaviors with them to show them you really care about them.

3. **In the future, ask for forgiveness from people you hurt and forgive those who have hurt you as soon as possible after the event.** It is inevitable that at some point you will hurt someone or others will hurt you. As soon as possible apologize to the person you hurt and forgive those who hurt you. Don't make excuses for you or them! Don't ask them to share the blame! Don't rehash the circumstances surrounding past hurtful interactions. Don't let the sun go down on any unforgiveness, however small. You will sleep better and trust more as a result.

"Be curious, not judgmental."
— Walt Whitman [31]

CHAPTER SEVEN: LESSONS LEARNED

- We are naturally tend to (pre)judge people and their ideas
- When we express our prejudices toward others we tell them we are more concerned with protecting our own (fragile) self-image than trying to understand what they have to say
- Psychologists suggest that when we judge we are probably self-incriminating
- Judgmental body language erodes speaker confidence and trust
- Being a devil's advocate is generally negative and destructive to communication.
- Often our self-righteousness attitude gets in the way of our listening
- Completely forgive those living and deceased who have hurt you
- Be extra careful not to hurt people during your healing process
- In the future, when you hurt someone tell them you are sorry and ask their forgiveness ASAP
- When someone hurts you in the future forgive them as soon as possible and *let it go*. You will sleep better and trust more as a result
- Don't let the sun go down on unforgiveness

CHAPTER 8

EMOTIONAL OVERDRIVE TO RELATIONSHIP INTELLIGENCE

"Feelings are much like waves, we can't stop them from coming but we can choose which one to surf."
— Jonatan Mårtensson

RELATIONSHIP INTELLIGENCE   SELF   OTHERS

6) When I am under extreme stress my listening behavior does not change   ____   ____
13) I plan ahead well to minimize stressful and/or emotional interactions   ____   ____
20) I control my emotions with difficult people and under trying circumstances   ____   ____

Averaged Totals   ____   ____
Grade   ____   ____

Rating Scale: 4 = Almost Always   3 = Most of the time   2 = Sometimes   1 = Seldom

Grade Ranges:
4.0-3.50: Exceptional   3.49-2.8: Good   2.7-2.3 Fair   2.2-below: Poor

---

I was recently forwarded the following email:

One day I hopped in a taxi and we took off for the airport. We were driving in the right lane when suddenly a black car jumped out of a parking space right in front of us. My taxi driver slammed on his brakes, skidded, and missed the other car by just inches! The driver of the other car whipped his head around and started yelling at us.

My taxi driver just smiled and waved at the guy. My taxi driver was really easy going and friendly. So I asked, 'Why did you just do that? That guy almost ruined your car and sent us to the hospital!' This is when my taxi driver taught me what I now call, **'The Law of the Garbage Truck.'**

You see, many people are like garbage trucks. They run around full of garbage, full of frustration, full of anger, and full of disappointment. As their container fills up, they need a place to dump their accumulated garbage and sometimes they'll dump it on me. I have learned not to take it personally.

I just smile, wave, wish them well, and move on. I own a taxi cab not a garbage truck. I don't want to take someone else's garbage and dump it on other people at work, at home, or in the street. The bottom line is that I don't let garbage trucks ruin my day.

1) Love the people who treat you right!
2) Pray for the ones who dump garbage on you!

Remember: Life is "Make it and Take it"!
Ten percent is what you "Make it" and ninety percent is how you "Take it!"

Have a garbage-free day!
– Anonymous

Wow! What a clever way to put the personal control we have over our responses to what people say and do to us and vice versa. We have a choice as to what we want to do with our own garbage and the garbage others *try* to dump on us, especially when one or all parties are on emotional overdrive. I suspect we all can come up with a plethora of examples where emotions, stress and mood state have altered our communication, especially our listening.

Think back even though it may be painful and explore examples of your worst interpersonal behavior. Recall when you have done things that have hurt others and/or yourself. Explore the circumstances surrounding these worst moments and how the stage was set for you to behave the way you did. I suggest that in most (if not all) cases you will find that your social misbehavior had something to do with your inability to handle your feelings and emotions at the time. When emotions are out of control your body chemistry (which is meant to protect you from danger) often causes you to lash out "in the heat of the moment." Sometimes your emotions have been brewing and stewing for quite a while and the behavior is a tipping point. Perhaps you were under significant stress at work and exploded when interacting with a family member (or the dog).

In his book, *Leading Minds* Howard Gardner refers to listening as "linguistic intelligence." Gardner believes we can learn to speak more effectively by improving our presentation skills. He is correct. I have taken such training and it has helped me tremendously as a presenter. However, as I confessed earlier, being a good presenter does not qualify me as a good listener. Relationship management is a better way to describe how we need to learn to communicate and improve our listening behavior. Stress, emotions and mood management depend on our ability to use our learned listening skills to focus on building mutually healthy and vibrant relationships.

TURNING PAIN INTO PEARLS

The most expensive cultured pearls are formed inside the shell of certain mollusks as a defense mechanism against a potentially threatening irritant, such as a parasite inside its shell, or an attack from outside, injuring the mantle tissue. The mollusk creates a pearl sac to seal off the irritation.

Like the mollusk we too can turn our irritation, pain and discomfort into valuable pearls based on how we respond physically and emotionally. Here is how your defensive chemistry works inside your body.

Your sympathetic nervous system does an excellent job of rapidly preparing you to deal with what you perceive as a threat to your safety. Your hormones trigger several metabolic reactions that best allow you to cope with apparent and sudden danger.

Your adrenal glands release adrenaline (also known as epinephrine) and other hormones that increase breathing, heart rate, and blood pressure. This moves more oxygen-rich blood faster to the brain and to the muscles needed for fighting or fleeing. And, you have plenty of energy to do either, because adrenaline causes a rapid release of glucose and fatty acids into your bloodstream. Also, your senses become keener, your memory sharper, and you are less sensitive to pain.

Other hormones shut down functions unnecessary during the emergency. Growth, reproduction, and the immune system all go on hold. Blood flow to the skin is reduced. That's why chronic stress often leads to sexual dysfunction, increases your chances of getting sick, and often manifests itself as skin ailments.

As you can see your body does a remarkable job of preparing you for imminent irritation, attack and/or pain. However it does you no favors where listening is concerned. Under stress your behavior naturally tends to become more aggressive, more extreme and increasingly hyper. Your ability to listen objectively is seriously impaired when extreme emotions and stress are part of the mix.

THE EMOTIONAL OVERDRIVE PROBLEM

Stress, mood and emotional state have the potential of dramatically changing our ability to be discerning as we attempt to communicate with others. When we are under extreme stress our entire body moves into a self-defense mode (mood) and our ability to listen effectively and objectively is severely hampered. Our natural tendency to experience different mood states and situational stress makes sustained effective listening difficult at best. Why? We are never so self-seeking as when we are protecting our emotional backside.

THE RADICAL RELATIONSHIP INTELLIGENCE SOLUTION

Our ability to communicate effectively is the most fundamental characteristic of building healthy relationships with others. Managing our emotions, stress and moods are critical if we wish to turn irritants into relationship pearls. I suggest that we need to develop and use "Relationship Intelligence" to catapult mind over matter. First we must assess our emotional strengths and weaknesses intimately. Then we need to manage the ongoing emotions and stress that are part and parcel of all relationships. We have the choice of cultivating pearls or throwing rocks. Relationship Intelligence is the process of applying radical servant listening to each unique relationship in our life regardless of the irritation and pressure to do otherwise. Relationship Intelligence is radical because it requires that you plan and strategize for *every relationship in your life,* from the least to the most important. We offer Relationship Intelligence tools and a website at the end of this book to help build your Relationship Intelligence. In the meantime, here are four ways to radically grow your Relationship Intelligence muscle:

1. **Be Proactive** by learning all you can about your own emotional strengths and weaknesses and how they affect each key relationship in your life. Ask others to do the same and then use your Relationship

Intelligence to anticipate the circumstances when either or both of you have been prone to interact based on emotion, stress or mood state. First come up with some ideas on how to avoid these circumstances all together.

2. **Relationships Trump Events.** Mutually pre-agree with each key person that your relationship is more important than any one circumstance and/or emotionally charged event. Mutually understand that you are going to make mistakes and let each other down. Most of these failures are what we call "minors." Big issues relating to deeper values, integrity and the like are called "majors." Agree to use your Relationship Intelligence to "major in the majors" and to "minor in the minors." Ask yourself this question when a potentially volatile situation comes up: *"Do I want to die now, on this hill?"* Is this a real "major" or is it a "minor?" Even if it is a "major" is this the time and place to go to battle? It takes an act of supernatural courage to avoid getting sucked into an emotional altercation when our hormones are raging and our defenses are fully engaged! If it is a major agree on the time and place for both parties to be at their problem-resolution best – not worst – especially where emotions are running hot. If it is a minor don't let your emotions turn a small flicker into a forest fire. In both cases use your Relationship Intelligence to deal with the issues later when emotions and circumstances are more positive and less volatile.

3. **Be Proactively Reactive** using your Relationship Intelligence and implement Advanced Warning systems that signal emotionally-charged behavior brewing and how best to respond. You may pre-agree that either party has the option of withdrawing from an interaction when they believe they may say or do something that might be harmful to the relationship. There may be certain sensitive words, phrases and references that you mutually pre-agree will not be used in the heat of battle. In the cool of pre-planning develop interaction ground rules that define how to interact positively and fight fairly.

4. By mutual pre-agreement bring a **Neutral Third Party** into certain interactions that have a history of volatility.

5. Combine a healthy **Diet and Regular Exercise** with actions 1-4 above to maximize your chances of developing and growing your Relationship

Intelligence with every relationship in your life. Diet and exercise have been linked to healthy brain function and effective stress management in a wide range of medical studies.

6. Learn how to **Crack the Listening Communication Code** covered in Chapters 9-15.

RELATED RADICAL LISTENERS' PLEDGE
I will listen with a sincere desire to be influenced.

CHAPTER EIGHT: LESSONS LEARNED

- Mood state, emotions and stress make listening more difficult
- Your nervous system and adrenal glands prepare you for perceived threat and pain
- Chronic stress response breaks down your immune system and your ability to listen
- Emotional overload tends to make you more reactive and defensive in your listening behavior
- Extreme mood swings break down interpersonal trust and communication potential
- You can use relationship challenges to cultivate pearls rather than throw rocks
- Relationship Intelligence integrates mind and body beginning with the sharing of information about you and others in order to create mutual understanding and trust
- "Major in the Majors" and "Minor in the Minors"
- Relationship Intelligence anticipates and sets up "Dos and Don'ts" for how two specific people should interact when one or both are experiencing extreme stress, emotion or mood state
- Healthy Diet and Exercise increase your chances of listening well under any circumstances due to optimal brain and body function

CHAPTER 9
TRANSITIONING FOREIGN TONGUE TO COMMON LANGUAGE

"A different language is a different vision of life."
— *Federico Fellini* [32]

COMMON TONGUE	SELF	OTHERS
7) I "get" the underlying meaning when others speak	⎯⎯	⎯⎯
14) I am good at putting myself in others' shoes as I listen to them	⎯⎯	⎯⎯
21) I flex well to the expectations of those speaking with me	⎯⎯	⎯⎯
Averaged Totals	⎯⎯	⎯⎯
Grade	⎯⎯	⎯⎯

Rating Scale: 4 = Almost Always 3 = Most of the time 2 = Sometimes 1 = Seldom

Grade Ranges:
4.0-3.50: Exceptional 3.49-2.8: Good 2.7-2.3 Fair 2.2-below: Poor

WHEN IN ROME DO AS THE ROMANS

In the movie classic *Tarzan*, a native hunk named Tarzan learns to communicate with a babe named Jane in their adventure with King Kong. They begin with words, grunts and gestures and learn to interact by trial and error. I suggest that when we listen to others the learning process is more Tarzan and Jane-like than we realize. If we take the time and go through the trials and errors eventually we can develop some rudimentary common language or language in common with others. This Tarzan-Jane trial and error phenomenon occurs in all relationships. Is it any wonder we can communicate at all knowing how different we all are due to widely differing genetics, experiences and different ways we speak and sometimes grunt?

I went to Germany years ago working with the Sheraton Corporation and their Frankfurt Germany based hotel leadership team. The team there all spoke English so I was able to complete our training activities quite successfully. When I left the English-speaking confines of the hotel I encountered people who were completely foreign to me. I was doing some pretty simple things like taking a cab, going to lunch, shopping, etc. What was most shocking to me was how utterly helpless I had become because I did not know how to speak their native tongue. The German vendors and people I encountered in the local community stretched to accommodate me but it was extremely uncomfortable for all parties. There I was, a Ph.D. in Human and Organization Development, and I felt like a complete moron. I was completely incapable of interacting effectively with people who only spoke German. Then I realized the obvious. If I was to communicate in a meaningful way with the Germans then I needed to crack the German communication code, i.e., I needed to learn how to listen and speak in German as well as in English. The other alternative was for the German people there to learn how to speak English so I could interact with them. Sound bizarre? Don't we sometimes expect others to think and speak like us and then get frustrated when they can't or won't?

My sister Mary Ann, a UC San Francisco pediatrician, and her daughters Julia and Elizabeth, cracked the French communication code by going to France. They immersed themselves in active relationships with French people in *their* culture for several years. I suggest that my sister and nieces learned to speak French differently than those who take a 90-day course. Why are these two approaches so different? Listening is being able to speak the language of those with whom you are communicating from their perspective.

In addition to cultural languages I have discovered that there are distinct communication languages and listening styles that transcend culture, dialect and idiom. My ongoing action research over the last 40 years suggests that each of us has learned and developed a unique communication language that allows us to *code* how we think, speak, listen and perceive the billions of external stimuli bombarding us daily. A unique language code stored in our schema library makes relative sense out of what we hear and how we speak.

Using a very large and continually expanding action research pool of participants we have discovered five distinguishably different Communication or Listening Languages, Styles or Codes. We naturally prefer to speak, think and listen in our own language. If we are to become a radically effective listener we need to be able to listen in and speak communication languages that are foreign and unnatural to us. Radical listening requires that we focus on specific people and the context of our relationship with them. Steven Covey suggests that we "seek first to understand and then to be understood." To understand others begins with Radical Servant

Listening, plain and simple. To be impactful with others we need to become fluent in their communication language in addition to our own.

THE RADICAL FOREIGN LANGUAGE PROBLEM

The natural way we build relationships with others is a trial-and-error process to develop a common communication lingo. We crack the code with some people fairly quickly, while with most people the communication trial-and-error process is more protracted, painful and difficult. Others in turn develop a simple code for understanding and communicating with us. The accuracy of these codes is often diminished when circumstances and emotions change.

Here is the problem! It is *not natural* to learn and speak in the preferred communication language of others. Even with those closest to us we struggle to understand their communication code and the underlying meaning of their words. We don't learn to think in their language nor do they learn to think in ours. We treat others around us like foreigners when it comes to communication. We tend to speak and think in our own tongue and expect others to adjust accordingly. It takes time and effort to learn another's communication language and we are too impatient to crack the communication code of another. Tarzan-Jane like communicating via trial and error takes time and effort so we tend to avoid it. As a result natural listening behavior is mostly hit or miss. With the best of intentions we end up falling way short when communicating with others because we don't speak their communication languages and they don't speak ours.

Without a doubt the most *radical* servant listening behavior is our ability to understand and then communicate with someone in their communication language. In my work I have been able to help people increase their listening effectiveness by teaching them how to *recognize and respond* to others using the Five Fundamental Listening Languages. Historically we have been taught the Golden Rule i.e., treat others the way we wish to be treated. This golden rule principle is often misunderstood and misapplied. Communicating with others in the way we like to be communicated to may work 20 percent of the time *at best*. I suggest that we need to communicate with others in a manner that works best for them first and often.

The impact of our genetics and experience on our ability to communicate effectively cannot be understated. By trial-and-error we become comfortable using a certain combination of communication behavior (schema processing). Over time we learn and hone our preferred lingo to the point that we can *speak it fluently.* The problem is that in order to communicate with others we need to understand *their* lingo in addition to our own.

This concept of adjusting yourself to others is very compatible with Ken Blanchard's *Situational Leadership® II* model where you adjust your leadership style to the person you are leading based on their stage of competency and maturity to do a particular assignment. [33] Ken suggests that flexibility is the key.

After adapting to the communications language of the subordinate, the servant leader should then recognize the subordinates' stage of development and adjust his/her leadership style accordingly. Similarly, Blanchard suggests that the Servant Leader adjust to his/her team's stage of development and adjust his/her team leadership behavior accordingly.

Gary Chapman suggests that each of us has a unique Love Language in his book *The Five Love Languages*.[34] Although words are used to express our love at times his reference to languages is more focused on behaviors than how we verbally communicate per se. He suggests that in intimate relationships we need to first identify the love language of our partner and then speak to them in that language as often as possible. This revolutionary approach puts a different spin on the Golden Rule and is the approach I have used with thousands of people over the last decade.

THE RADICAL CODE BREAKING SOLUTION:

1. Objectively Assess your Listening Strengths and Weaknesses:
   a) Complete the Listening Assessment and see where you need to grow the most.
   b) Read Chapters 10-15 to understand how communication languages work.
   c) Informally determine your own communication language including your listening strengths and weaknesses.
   d) Take a Communication Language assessment for more information about what makes you tick as a communicator. See appendix for instructions on taking *The INTRPLAY Communications DNA Profile*.

2. **Recognize and Respond using Others' Communication Language.** Learn to communicate in the lingo of those around you. Use the information in Chapters 10 to 15 to learn how to communicate in the Five Communication Languages.

3. **Do Relationship Transformation (Chapter 16).**
   Start with your Key Relationships and then branch out to others.

4. **Complete the Call to Action (Chapter 17).**
   Walk the talk of servant listening, one servant listening behavior at a time.

RELATED RADICAL LISTENERS' PLEDGE
I will respond to others with an encouraging spirit.

CHAPTER NINE: LESSONS LEARNED

- Most people learn and prefer to use one of Five Communication Languages almost exclusively when interacting with others
- Learning a new communication language can be as painful and difficult as learning how to speak German, French or Russian
- Natural communication is a Tarzan-Jane like trial-and-error process often requiring time, patience and persistence to achieve basic effectiveness
- Most relationship problems are compounded if not caused by the inability of the parties to communicate effectively in each others' communication language
- The first step in communication code-breaking is to learn more about our own communication preferences including both our communication strengths and weaknesses
- Chapters 10 to 15 cover the how-to for each of the Five Communication Languages
- If we are to truly understand others we need to quickly learn to decode and then communicate in a lingo and manner that works for them
- Radical servant listening is the ability to recognize and respond to others using the Five Listening Languages

CHAPTER 10
RECOGNIZING AND RESPONDING TO LISTENING LANGUAGES

"A person hears only what they understand."
— *Johann Wolfgang Von Goethe* [35]

Before we get into the details of the Five Communication Languages here are some basics on the power of individual differences in shaping how we communicate, especially how we listen. We are different from one another in so many ways: shape, size, weight, ethnicity, gender, amount of hair on our head, educational level, financial worth, foods we enjoy, hobbies, sports we follow, what we read, how we use our free time, occupation, faith, age, ad infinitum.

In our research into communication languages and listening we discovered that there are two general differences preferences that tend to define our communication languages and behavior. Each of these differences can be described on a continuum from one extreme to another:

1) *Preference for Deliberate* is on one extreme and *Preference for Fast Pace* is on the other extreme. Again, most of us would fall somewhere in between. See Fig. 1.
2) *Task Preference* is on one extreme and *People Preference* is on the other. Each of us therefore would fall somewhere in between. See Fig. 2.

The Five Communication Languages Model in Fig. 3 integrates these two scales.

CRACKING THE RADICAL SERVANT LISTENING CODE

Imagine that you are able to decode any combination to any safe where untold treasure is stored up and waiting for you. The only catch is that you need to *know the combination* to the safe. Look at each person in your life, especially those closest to you as having incredible treasure stored up inside begging to be shared. Your challenge is that each person *has a different combination* to their safe. What opens the safe for your boss does not work for a co-worker. What works for your spouse does not necessarily work for your teenager. What works with one client does not work for another.

In the next five chapters we will show you how to crack the code that opens the safe for all the people in your life – present and future – if you learn and apply our code-cracking tools correctly. In order to truly understand how to listen and how to respond to others we need the combinations to the safes around us. We call this process "cracking the listening code." Each Communication/Listening Language has its own unique code. In the chapters that follow we will show you how to crack each listening code beginning first with your own. These codes will help you unlock the communication safe, so to speak. Code cracking allows others to feel safe sharing openly and honestly with you and vice versa.

In addition to powerful tools to improve your listening and communication with others, we will help you use these tools to become a servant listener. You will learn to listen in the communication languages of others. You will have the opportunity to acquire a "heart condition" so that you can care about what is best for others. The effectiveness of these tools we are sharing with you hinges on your ability to develop the heart condition of a servant listener. To be a credible servant listener we show you the combinations that unlock the Five Communication and Listening Languages. Here are some basics to keep in mind as you master communication linguistics.

RADICAL SERVANT LISTENING FUNDAMENTALS

1) There are no good or bad, right or wrong listening languages!
2) Each of us is a combination, more or less, of all Five Listening Languages
3) What makes us each unique is how and when and what listening languages we use in the service of others.
4) At any particular time we can use any combination of listening languages.
5) Our extensive research shows that each of us enjoys behaving in our *preferred* area of communication and listening. Our communication comfort zone can encompass any combination of listening languages but normally one stands out above the others.
6) Extreme circumstances and/or stress tend to change our behavior in that situation.
7) Responding to others in their listening language tends to build relationship trust, openness and effectiveness *IF* done with an empathetic *heart condition.*

We begin our decoding process with some basics on individual differences and how to Recognize and Respond to the Five Communication Languages. (Fig. 4 & 5)

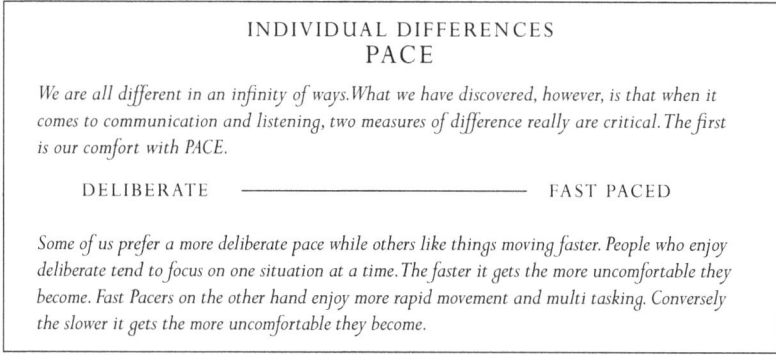

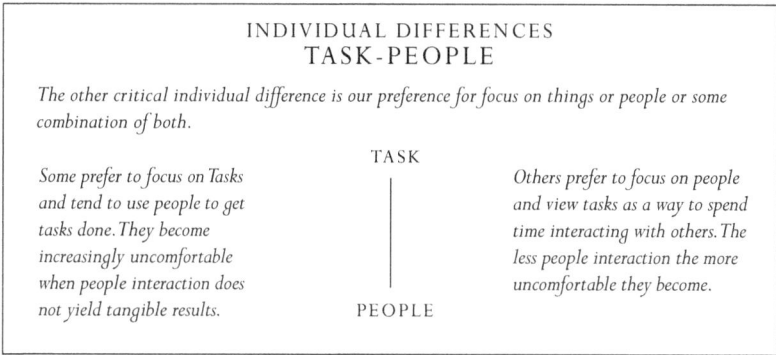

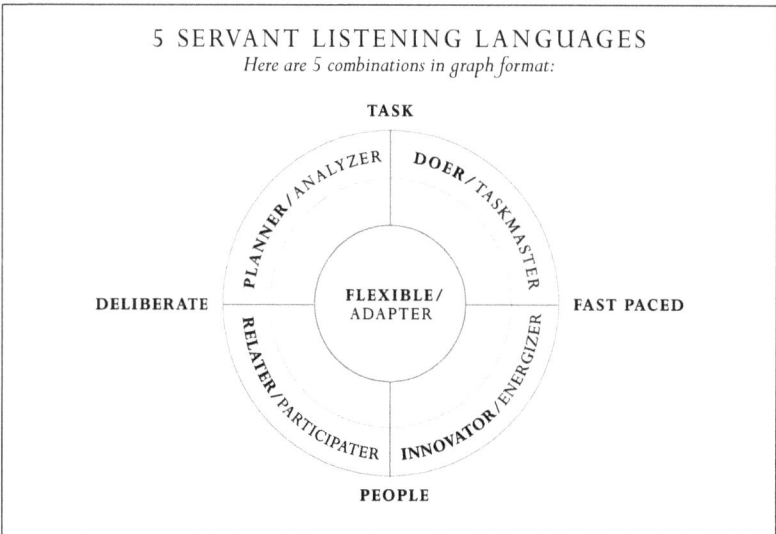

INDIVIDUAL DIFFERENCES
PACE

We are all different in an infinity of ways. What we have discovered, however, is that when it comes to communication and listening, two measures of difference really are critical. The first is our comfort with PACE.

DELIBERATE ——————————— FAST PACED

Some of us prefer a more deliberate pace while others like things moving faster. People who enjoy deliberate tend to focus on one situation at a time. The faster it gets the more uncomfortable they become. Fast Pacers on the other hand enjoy more rapid movement and multi tasking. Conversely the slower it gets the more uncomfortable they become.

FIGURE 1

INDIVIDUAL DIFFERENCES
TASK-PEOPLE

The other critical individual difference is our preference for focus on things or people or some combination of both.

TASK

Some prefer to focus on Tasks and tend to use people to get tasks done. They become increasingly uncomfortable when people interaction does not yield tangible results.

Others prefer to focus on people and view tasks as a way to spend time interacting with others. The less people interaction the more uncomfortable they become.

PEOPLE

FIGURE 2

5 SERVANT LISTENING LANGUAGES
Here are 5 combinations in graph format:

FIGURE 3

Fig. 4 below is an overview of how to *recognize* the Five Distinct Servant Listening Languages. Fig. 5 is an overview of how to *respond* to the Five Distinct Servant Listening Languages:

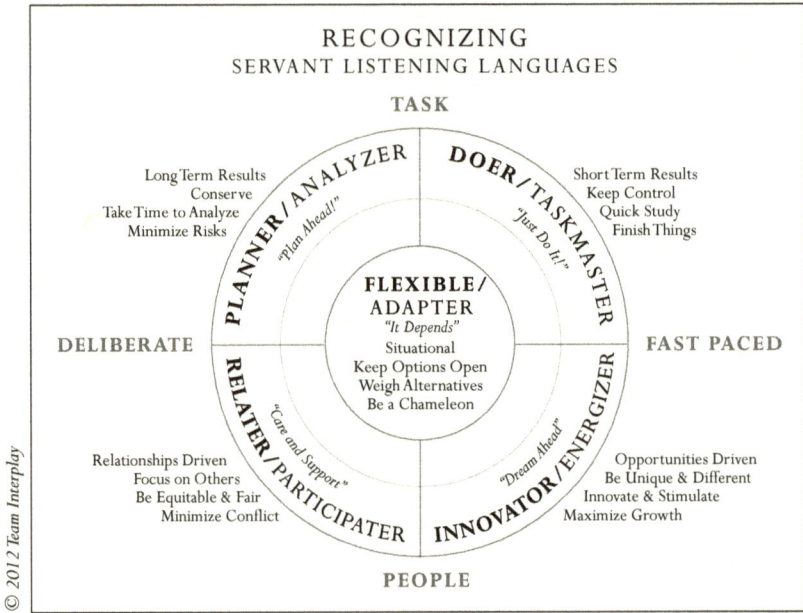

RECOGNIZING
SERVANT LISTENING LANGUAGES

TASK

PLANNER / ANALYZER
"Plan Ahead!"

Long Term Results
Conserve
Take Time to Analyze
Minimize Risks

DOER / TASKMASTER
"Just Do It!"

Short Term Results
Keep Control
Quick Study
Finish Things

FLEXIBLE/ ADAPTER
"It Depends"
Situational
Keep Options Open
Weigh Alternatives
Be a Chameleon

DELIBERATE

FAST PACED

RELATER / PARTICIPATER
"Care and Support"

Relationships Driven
Focus on Others
Be Equitable & Fair
Minimize Conflict

INNOVATOR / ENERGIZER
"Dream Ahead"

Opportunities Driven
Be Unique & Different
Innovate & Stimulate
Maximize Growth

PEOPLE

© 2012 Team Interplay

FIGURE 4

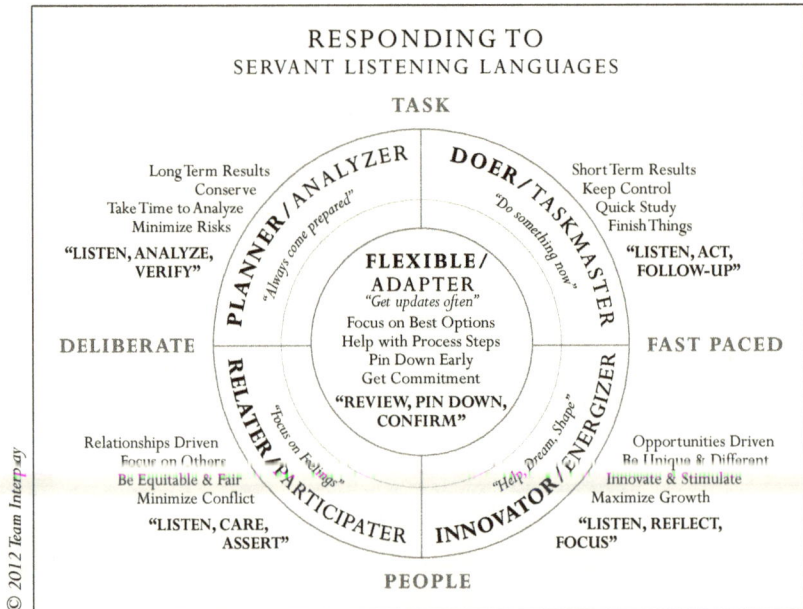

RESPONDING TO
SERVANT LISTENING LANGUAGES

TASK

PLANNER / ANALYZER
"Always come prepared"

Long Term Results
Conserve
Take Time to Analyze
Minimize Risks

"LISTEN, ANALYZE, VERIFY"

DOER / TASKMASTER
"Do something now"

Short Term Results
Keep Control
Quick Study
Finish Things

"LISTEN, ACT, FOLLOW-UP"

FLEXIBLE/ ADAPTER
"Get updates often"
Focus on Best Options
Help with Process Steps
Pin Down Early
Get Commitment
"REVIEW, PIN DOWN, CONFIRM"

DELIBERATE

FAST PACED

RELATER / PARTICIPATER
"Focus on feelings"

Relationships Driven
Focus on Others
Be Equitable & Fair
Minimize Conflict

"LISTEN, CARE, ASSERT"

INNOVATOR / ENERGIZER
"Help Dream, Shape"

Opportunities Driven
Be Unique & Different
Innovate & Stimulate
Maximize Growth

"LISTEN, REFLECT, FOCUS"

PEOPLE

© 2012 Team Interplay

FIGURE 5

Fig. 6 is a **Quick Reference Power Tool** to help you to compare and contrast the different Servant Listening languages and how best to be effective interacting with each language.

SERVANT LISTENING LANGUAGES
Recognize and Respond Chart

Language	Recognize	Respond	Strengths	Blind Spots
TASKMASTER	Results Driven Bottom Line Crisp and Clear Works Hard	Agree on Goals Cut to the Chase Be Specific Offer to Help	Does things Stays Focused Persistent Low Maintain	Conditional Closed Insensitive Impatient
ANALYZER	Data Driven Quality Focused Systematic Risk Minimizer	Use Facts Prepare & Plan Standardize Give Pros/Cons	Accurate Logical Organized Realistic	Over Analyzes Narrow Skeptical Not Creative
PARTICIPATOR	Relates Well Interactive Supportive Trusting	Be Open Be Sincere Empathize Personalize	Caring Comfortable Listens Well Loyal	Avoids Conflict Unassertive Sensitive Touchy-feely
ENERGIZER	Change Driven Possibilities Sells/Promotes Creative	Be Responsive Brainstorm Offer Support Help to Focus	Creative Visionary Inspirational Change Agent	Impractical Idealistic Conceptual Not Detailed
FLEXIBLE *Taskmaster* *Analyzer* *Participator* *Energizer*	Options Driven "It Depends" Situational Unpredictable	Pin Down Clarify & Focus Prioritize Be Decisive	Change Agent Adaptable Responsive Fluid	Non-committal Unfocused Unrealistic Ambiguous

FIGURE 6

Let's now look at how the Five Servant Listening Languages work to make you a servant listener. Chapter 11 will give you a deeper understanding of how to *recognize* and *respond* to the TASKMASTER/DOER.

CHAPTER 11
TASKMASTER/DOER

"If we try to listen we find it extraordinarily difficult, because we are always projecting our opinions and ideas, our prejudices, our background, our inclinations, our impulses; when they dominate, we hardly listen at all to what is being said.... One listens and therefore learns, only in a state of silence, in which this whole background is in abeyance, is quiet; then, it seems to me, it is possible to communication."
— *Jiddu Krishnamurti* [36]

Our first code breaking venture is with the TASKMASTER/DOER. Approximately 20 percent of those with whom you will interact will prefer to use this communication language. The percentage of Taskmaster/Doers jumps to over 40 percent among team and business leaders using our assessment tools.

CRACKING THE TASKMASTER/DOER LISTENING CODE

A great example of a Taskmaster/Doer is Richard Blackaby. I was introduced to Richard several years ago by Vince Siciliano one of our original INTRPLAY Profile facilitators. I was humbled when I met Richard by all he had on his plate as: the President of Blackaby Ministries International; a sought-after speaker on Christian leadership and spirituality, an author and a husband, father and son. I have an expression I often use that aptly fits Richard: "He is one of the busiest men on the planet."

Richard completed the Communications INTRPLAY Profile and I asked him to review the results and highlight some "sticky" words that accurately described him. Here is what he replied:

Words that "stick" with me are: results, quick decisions, self motivated achievers, doers.

The opposite for me is "hand holding" – that is, having to keep nursing along people who are being paid to get results. I am happy with providing needed supplies or answering legitimate questions, but don't resonate with people who need to be constantly motivated when they are on the team.

Richard, like most Taskmaster/Doers, is sincere in his relationships but his main focus is on producing and performing with quality and quantity. You have to earn the right to be trusted by Richard and other Taskmaster/Doers. That earned trust comes only one way: by successful performance that sustains over time.

Here are two of Richard's defining moments that clearly demonstrate the strengths and challenges of the Taskmaster/Doer:

Moment #1: After a year or two of marriage, Lisa, my wife, who is an extreme feeler, tried to get through to me. She presented a problem to me that seemed easily solvable. I didn't understand why she was stuck on something that I could solve in a few minutes. It finally dawned on me that her "presenting problem" was not her real problem. I was so oriented to quick problem solving that I had not probed more deeply to discover her "real" problem. From my perspective, I did not understand why someone would not just say what their problem was. It seemed to me like game playing to present a surface issue when someone's real issue was much deeper. In retrospect, I was acting and thinking like a "results oriented" Taskmaster/Doer and she was acting and thinking like a "sensing and feeling" Participator/ Relater.

What I learned in that moment about Lisa has helped me and us in our ongoing relationship:

1) At times Lisa doesn't truly understand her deeper issues. She comes to me for help to uncover issues not to "fix them" for her. In the past I had been focusing on the problem solution but she needed help in understanding the deeper issue. I learned that at these times she needs me to be a facilitator.

2) I also learned in that moment that I need to communicate with Lisa using her communication language i.e., as a Participator/Relater. Lisa needs to know that I am a sympathetic and empathetic listener before she will trust me with her deepest hurts.

Moment #2: I was the CEO of a graduate school when some key stakeholders made some sweeping changes that dramatically affected our school. I was upset and my immediate response was to dump my displeasure on my stakeholder liaison. I realized later that he was on my side. After my diatribe he had agreed with my position and wanted to help me. Instead of spewing I should have just asked him about his reactions and then just listened. I could have saved us both some unpleasant moments.

What I learned was not to make quick assumptions about people before asking them questions first. In retrospect I believe my Taskmaster/Doer impatience took over and prevented me from listening to my liaison. As a result, I have tried to ask more questions and listen more before responding in all my interactions.

Richard then shared his experiences with some great listeners in his life:

One great listener who has impacted my life greatly is my dad, Henry. I have always been impressed with how he has such wisdom to share. He listens to what I say and then he always makes his words count. He doesn't necessarily say a lot, but what he says is always profound.

I have had a 2-3 colleagues over the years that have impressed me with their listening ability. Every time I am with them I find myself talking more about myself than I intended to. They just naturally ask good questions and demonstrate genuine interest and concern. I find having a lunch with them extremely therapeutic. I have had a couple of people like that over my career. There aren't many like them but they stand out. When you are going through a difficult or complex time, they are the ones you want to get with as soon as you can.

Here is how Richard views the "servant listener:"

I believe the servant listener is someone who asks perceptive, life-opening questions and then truly listens until he/she understands. The servant listener has the ability to communicate their genuine concern and empathy for you regardless of the circumstances. The servant listener is a facilitator of understanding.

RECOGNIZING AND RESPONDING

You can recognize the Taskmaster/Doer (TD) in Fig. 7 because they are the most obvious of the listening languages. Pleasure for the TD is anything associated with control, results, bottom line, short-term perspective, immediate action and/or problem resolution. The Taskmaster/Doer tends to experience pain and discomfort with people and things that: move slowly, get "touchy-feely," involve extreme emotions and don't appear to address what he or she thinks is most important at the time.

If you want to crack the TD code then focus on learning to responding to the Taskmaster/Doer using Fig. 8. Remember the TD thinks in seconds

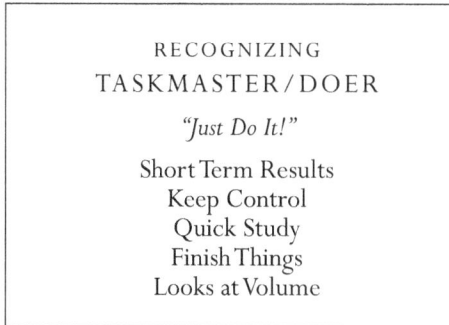

RECOGNIZING
TASKMASTER/DOER

"Just Do It!"

Short Term Results
Keep Control
Quick Study
Finish Things
Looks at Volume

FIGURE 7

not minutes, hours, days, weeks, months or even years. The "here and now" is where they are and you can't get things done too quickly to suit them. Find out what is most important *to them* and their expectations as to how you can help. Agree on expected deliverables and measures. Spell out roles and activities and how you will measure results. Remember your goal is to work on the Taskmaster's goal. By so doing you earn the TD's respect and trust which will be critical if you desire to have the TD help you with your priorities and agenda.

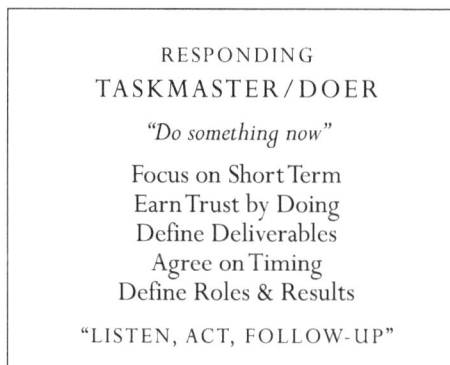

RESPONDING
TASKMASTER/DOER

"Do something now"

Focus on Short Term
Earn Trust by Doing
Define Deliverables
Agree on Timing
Define Roles & Results

"LISTEN, ACT, FOLLOW-UP"

FIGURE 8

Listening Tips for the Taskmaster/Doer are summarized below. Communication Dos and Don'ts are summarized in Fig. 9.

RADICAL LISTENING WHEN INTERACTING WITH A TASKMASTER/DOER

- Allow the Taskmaster to be in control
- Listen for the "expected results" and measures
- Don't socialize unless the Taskmaster initiates
- Identify potential barriers and possible ways to overcome
- Ask Taskmaster how you can help
- Agree on your and others' roles
- Be direct in working out any concerns or differences
- Let the Taskmaster summarize key points
- Mutually develop an Action Plan
- Give each other continual written feedback
- Meet briefly but regularly and adjust as you go

COMMUNICATION TIPS
if you are a Taskmaster

TASKMASTER interacting with a:	Dos	Don'ts	Maximizing your impact as a TASKMASTER
TASKMASTER	Collaborate on Agendas Agree on Priorities Focus on Time Lines Define Accountabilities	Compete Force or Intimidate Marginalize Be Condescending	Define Who is in Control of What Early Keep it Short and Simple Look for Win-Win Solutions Agree on Follow-Up Process
ANALYZER	Define Expectations Share Details Agree on a Plan Be Patient	Ignore Key Details Force or Bully Marginalize Facts Be Pushy	Show Analyzer you are Competent Overkill Who, What, When, Where, How Push the Analyzer to be more Timely Be Proactive about Critical Data
PARTICIPATOR	Define Customer Needs Share True Feelings Focus on People Slow Down and Listen	Drive your Agenda Marginalize Concerns Confront Be Disrespectful	Let the Participator be in Control Emphasize Benefits to People Mutually Agree on Expected Outcomes Mutually Define Measures of Success
ENERGIZER	Define Desired Outcome Think Outside the Box Focus on Bigger Picture Define Accountabilities	Shoot Down Ideas Interrupt Be Self-Serving Stay too Conceptual	Praise the Energizer's Unique Abilities Focus on New Solutions to Old Issues Synergize and Take Action Define Deliverables & Follow-Up
FLEXIBLE *Taskmaster* *Analyzer* *Participator* *Energizer*	Limit Alternatives Get Focused Early Define Mutual Needs Manage Change	Be too Flexible Be Indecisive Be Hard to Read Wait too Long to make Decisions	Determine Flexible's Current DNA Confirm Priorities Continually Define Conditions Constantly Check in Frequently Stick to Mutual Goals

FIGURE 9

CHAPTER 12
ANALYZER/PLANNER

"Wisdom is the reward you get for a lifetime when you'd rather have been talking."
— *Aristotle*

Approximately 10 percent of those with whom you interact will be the ANALYZER/PLANNER. Colonel L.C. aka "The Colonel" is our Analyzer/ Planner who served the majority of his professional career with the U.S. Army Corps of Engineers in various worldwide assignments including Vietnam. In addition to commanding troop at many levels, the Colonel was a Project Leader and Engineer supervising technical work teams. Now retired, the Colonel is an engineering consultant to various construction companies and government agencies. Here are some excerpts from a recent interview with the Colonel:

The Analyzer/Planner description fits me quite well. The words from my profile that stick with me are the need for facts, details and data. I need to study things first to make sure I am competent in my subsequent actions and recommendations. I listen mostly for hard data and more selectively for feelings and intangibles. Other sticky words are quality and timeliness. I enjoy teaching and coaching willing listeners who pay attention to detail like I do. I try to balance my passion for task work with trusted people interactions. I am least comfortable with rapid responses without accuracy and when working on ambiguous activities. When I am stressed out I seek out those I trust the most and become a selective listener with everyone else. I also tend to cope with stress by becoming more of a micro manager.

When I was asked to think back about the defining moments in my life I completely blanked out on my early childhood from birth through high school. After some reflection I realize now why I tend to have early childhood memory gap. I grew up in a highly dysfunctional family and my early family life was so out of control, unpredictable and painful I believe I have tried to erase most of it from my memory to minimize the hurt. One of the by-products of being an adult child of an alcoholic is that I have had issues with control most of my life. My early childhood has affected how I communicate, how I listen and how I interact with family, friends and others. I learned early in my life how to erect walls around me to avoid the pain of listening. I learned to be creative in how I looked at situations often changing the details to make my perceived reality more palatable than the real one.

At some level my childhood had a bearing on my career choice going from a life where nothing was under my control to a life where just about everything was either in a manual or regimented one way or another. I am fascinated with engineering, construction and problem solving because I get immersed in technical data and information. I enjoy working with my team to accomplish tangible results. I tend to listen like an engineer professionally but become more selective with others when feelings and emotions are involved especially with my family.

One of my defining moments was joining the International Twelve Step Fellowship: Al-Anon. Here I had a chance to understand that I was not the only one trying to cope with the pain caused by the disease of alcoholism. For the first time I had people around me to help me deal with my pain and I had a chance to help them with theirs. Finally I could share my painful feelings and emotions that had been bottled up inside me since childhood. I continue to attend Al-Anon meetings to help in my recovery. I continue to learn how to listen to others with compassion and care and to let go of guilt and fear. Al-Anon helped me to listen and to learn from my body and from my God. To help me day by day, I use the acronym HALT which are the first letters of the words: Hungry, Angry, Lonely, or Tired. When I am feeling the strain of any combination of these four conditions I stop what I am doing and take care of myself. When I am healthy and more balanced I am better able to listen well and serve others.

I believe the servant listener is someone who will take the time to understand others' needs, wants and expectations. I tend to struggle with patience as people unfold their issues and problems because I love to jump in and "solve their problem". As a part of my growth as a servant listener, I am working on letting people complete their thoughts and sentences before saying or doing anything. Throughout my career others have expected me to be the "answer man" and I have enjoyed playing that role. I know the servant listener must have a heart condition for people and I now try to balance my heart and my head when it comes to working with others. I realize now I don't have to be in charge or have to tell people what to do to be an effective leader. I am learning that others don't really want an "answer man" as much as someone just to listen to what they have to say with a humble heart.

I have recently learned to listen in others' communication language but tend to struggle with speaking it. My need for perfection often inhibits my ability to listen with an open mind and humble heart. My most helpful new listening behavior is to let others speak first and to pause before responding. I hope you will be encouraged by my ongoing transformation from a DOER driven to LISTENER driven. I also hope you begin transforming your listening behavior as soon as possible. Please note I have not included my full name because I have pledged not to reveal publicly any of my experiences with Al-Anon where meetings are conducted in complete safety and anonymity.

Everything I have shared above is true and from my heart. I share my story so that you may have hope that you can overcome *anything* that is limiting you. All you need to do is to become a Radical Listener with the realization you can't do it alone.

RECOGNIZING AND RESPONDING

As you will see in Fig. 10, you can recognize the Analyzer/Planner (AP) because they are the ones who ask the most detailed questions! The AP experiences pleasure with data, information, processes, procedures, probabilities and/or anything tangible that defines how things are quantified or standardized. The AP on the other hand tends to experience pain and discomfort with people and things that are fast moving, undefined, continually changing, conceptual and/or requiring creativity without documentation.

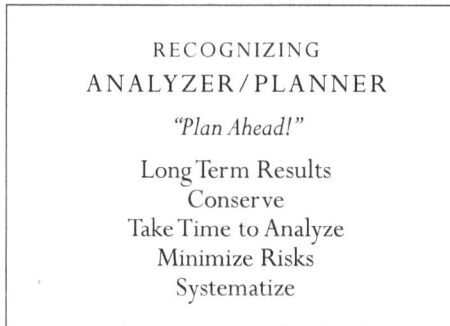

RECOGNIZING
ANALYZER/PLANNER

"Plan Ahead!"

Long Term Results
Conserve
Take Time to Analyze
Minimize Risks
Systematize

FIGURE 10

As summarized in Fig. 11, if you want to crack the Analyzer/Planner code then focus on being competent in all your interactions with them. Bring facts and details not emotions as you emphasize doing things right the first time. Quality and details make their day! You have to earn the AP's trust over time and multiple interactions. Planning is one of their favorite activities so learn how they do it. Where the Taskmaster/Doer processes things in minutes, seconds and sometimes nanoseconds, the Analyzer/Planner frames time in days, weeks and months. *Doing the right things right* is their mantra. Agree on *how* things will be done and measured. Clarify roles and the process steps to accomplish those goals. Remember you need to earn the AP's trust so allow them to be in control. Remember to use the Analyzer/Planner communication language as often as possible when dealing with them.

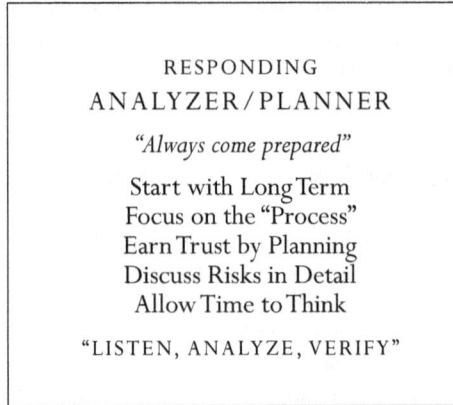

RESPONDING

ANALYZER / PLANNER

"Always come prepared"

Start with Long Term
Focus on the "Process"
Earn Trust by Planning
Discuss Risks in Detail
Allow Time to Think

"LISTEN, ANALYZE, VERIFY"

FIGURE 11

Listening Tips for the Analyzer/Planner are summarized below.
Communication Dos and Don'ts are summarized in Fig. 12 (page 62).

RADICAL LISTENING WHEN INTERACTING WITH AN ANALYZER/PLANNER

- Take notes and document everything
- Listen for Analyzer's concerns and objectives
- Probe for required details
- Identify credible and not credible information sources
- Distinguish between facts and opinions
- Identify potential barriers and use a problem solving process
- Work out any concerns/differences in detail
- Ask Analyzer to summarize key points and clarify
- Agree on your roles and the roles of others
- Develop an action plan
- Give each other continual written feedback
- Meet intermittently to adjust to new information and details

COMMUNICATION TIPS
if you are an Analyzer/Planner

ANALYZER interacting with a:	*Dos*	*Don'ts*	*Maximizing your impact as an* **ANALYZER**
TASKMASTER	Speak/Write in Bullets Agree on Priorities Identify Needed Info Focus on Time lines	Overload on Details Be a Word Smith Criticize Be Easily Offended	Let the Taskmaster be in Control State your Needs in Bullets Negotiate Win-Win Solutions Agree on Follow-Up Steps
ANALYZER	Share Facts/Details Agree on Priorities Develop the Plan Implement the Plan	Procrastinate Miss the Point Overanalyze Be Compulsive	Show the Analyzer you are Competent Agree on Goals First Agree on the Steps/Process Measure and Report Regularly
PARTICIPATOR	Identify your Customer Share Feelings/Needs Focus on Key Facts Include Key People	Overload with Details Marginalize People Be Insincere Be Impatient	Encourage the Participator to Share Relate Actions to Benefits Be Low Key and Others-Oriented Mutually Define Measures of Success
ENERGIZER	Define Desired Outcome Stretch Outside the Box Begin with Agreements Be Enthusiastic	Say "Can't" Be a Know-It-All Be too Formal Be Inflexible	Praise the Energizer's Unique Abilities Focus on Simple Steps First Agree on Who Does What Follow-Up Frequently
FLEXIBLE *Taskmaster* *Analyzer* *Participator* *Energizer*	Limit Alternatives Get Focused Early Define Mutual Needs Manage Change	Be too Flexible Be Indecisive Be Hard to Read Wait too Long to Make Decisions	Determine Flexible's Current DNA Confirm Priorities Continually Define Conditions Constantly Check in Frequently Stick to Mutual Goals

FIGURE 12

CHAPTER 13
PARTICIPATOR/RELATER

"Flatter me, and I may not believe you. Criticize me, and I may not like you. Ignore me, and I may not forgive you. Encourage me, and I will not forget you. Love me and I may be forced to love you."
— *William Arthur Ward* [37]

Now let's get a feel for the Listening Language with the largest following. PARTICIPATOR/RELATER'S comprise about 35 percent of the population. My Participator/Relater example is Robert Jackson. Rob was the 2011 North Carolina Principal of the Year based on his incredible work as the founding principal for Cuthbertson High School in Waxhaw NC where my daughter Christen attended for two years and just graduated. I had the pleasure of interacting with Rob during Christen's junior and senior year and struck up a friendship with him (as he is very prone to do with people).

In response to what he found "sticky" about the profile, he shared, "My leadership style is relational above all things. I seek to develop relationships with all those with whom I come into contact."

Here is how Rob describes how he uses his Participator/Relater style in his principal's role:

I am asked to fill countless roles in the school from managing administrators and teachers to building operations. My most crucial role however is being the learning community's greatest cheerleader. I try to encourage every child in my care to reach his/her potential. I encourage and coach teachers as they do the hard work of building and implementing great instructional activities. I attempt to motivate all of the learners (children and adults) on campus to continue to seek excellence in every aspect of their journey. I am passionate about parents working with their own children and as they volunteer in the organizations crucial to a school's success (Parent-Teacher Organizations, Athletic and Band Booster Clubs). In this role of "cheerleader," I keep all the stakeholders up to speed on progress toward key vision and mission milestones as well as recognizing the little things that often go unnoticed. I am constantly checking in with students and teachers. When I ask "How are you," they know that I sincerely want to know the answer because I care about each of them.

As the Founding Principal of a brand-new high school, I have worked hard to create a culture of caring, a natural outgrowth of my preferred Listening Language. My job is to Listen to People around me and then to respond appropriately. I try to be a servant leader at all times in every relationship by listening first and caring much. I try to be a partner with students and staff to overcome barriers and find resources. Our school has received the state's highest academic designation, "NC Honor School of Excellence" each year that we have been open. Our teachers have been honored as District Teacher of the Year and County Teacher of the Year both years which is an amazing feat in a district with 53 schools. The athletic teams have won conference, regional, and state championships. The band has filled trophy cases with the results of their contests. Yet in this place of great success, with stories abounding of excellence in action, the story that I hold closest to my heart is one of three students who had previously experienced rampant failure in school.

The three students arrived at Cuthbertson when we opened from very different places. Yet, each had one thing in common, a pattern of repeated academic failure. Each should have graduated the previous year, but they found themselves in a new school classified as juniors. Their grade placement was telling. Each had heard from their previous school that they had no chance of graduating and that they were being sent to a new school that did not even have a senior class because not only would they not graduate, they would not be able to earn enough credits to be re-classified as seniors during the year. First of all I wanted to hear their individual stories from their own lips. I then pushed and encouraged them. Teachers and I huddled with them and helped them successfully complete online classes at night. When they felt like giving up or walking away, we were there to pat them on the back, to listen as they related how hard their journey was, and to cheer them back onto the right path. At the end of the year, they had each earned the credits they needed to not only be classified as seniors, but to graduate as well.

Their graduation was a defining moment for me. By listening intently and by showing I cared for the three students and their teachers, I experienced every educator's dream, helping a student earn success they themselves did not think was possible.

At the banquet in the State Capital, as I heard my name being called out as the new State Principal of the Year, I was humbled thinking of all the students, teachers, administrators and parents who made this moment possible. As a Participator/Relater, my life as a servant leader is all about building healthy relationships. My true rewards are not the accolades but in seeing others grow and succeed as the result of my relationship with them.

"Few people are successful unless other people want them to be."
— Charlie Brown

RECOGNIZING AND RESPONDING

As you will see in Fig. 13, you can recognize the Participator/Relater because they are the ones who seem to enjoy being around certain people or people in general. The Participator/Relater tends to experience pleasure being around certain people or people in general. They enjoy openness, trust, relationships, feelings and/or emotions except for anger. The PR tends to experience pain and discomfort with conflict/confrontation, fast movement without sufficient involvement and/or anything that they perceive could be potentially damaging to themselves or the people/relationships around them.

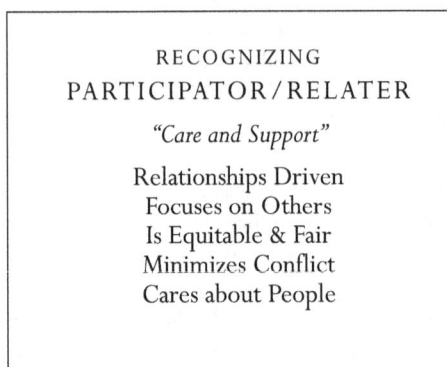

RECOGNIZING

PARTICIPATOR / RELATER

"Care and Support"

Relationships Driven
Focuses on Others
Is Equitable & Fair
Minimizes Conflict
Cares about People

FIGURE 13

If you want to crack the Participator/Relater code then examine Fig. 14. You must focus on being sincere and relational in all your interactions with them. Be willing to mutually share true emotions and feelings as you interact. Pay attention to the impact ideas and suggestions have on the PR's key stakeholders. Fairness and equitable treatment are paramount. PRs also avoid conflict and confrontation as much as possible so listen for ways to unite and collaborate. Caring for others is their mantra. Agree on who will be involved and affected and then how things will be done. Clarify roles to insure that all parties are plugged in and supportive. Remember you need to earn the AP's trust by building positive relationships, mutual trust and hope for the future. See Fig. 15 for specific Do's and Don'ts for cracking the Participator code.

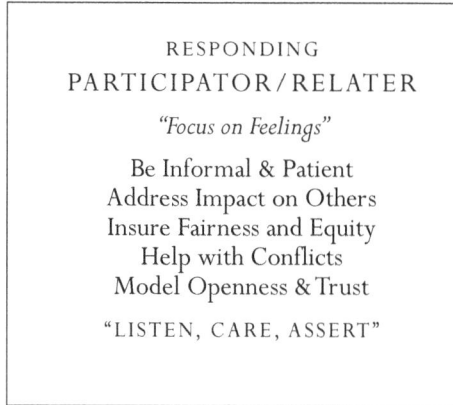

```
┌─────────────────────────────────┐
│          RESPONDING             │
│    PARTICIPATOR / RELATER       │
│                                 │
│        "Focus on Feelings"      │
│                                 │
│      Be Informal & Patient      │
│     Address Impact on Others    │
│     Insure Fairness and Equity  │
│        Help with Conflicts      │
│      Model Openness & Trust     │
│                                 │
│     "LISTEN, CARE, ASSERT"      │
│                                 │
└─────────────────────────────────┘
```

FIGURE 14

Listening Tips for the Participator/Relater are summarized below.
Communication Dos and Don'ts are summarized in Fig. 15.

RADICAL LISTENING WHEN INTERACTING WITH A PARTICIPATOR / RELATER

- Establish a friendly rapport without coming across as "glad handing"
- Listen for the Participator's true feelings and concerns about others
- Probe for people-related issues, opportunities and challenges
- Identify friends and relationships in common that you both trust
- You need to be authentic that you care about the Participator and others
- Identify any problem areas and who is involved
- Be continually aware of the impact of decisions on all stakeholders
- Ask the Participator how you can help
- Agree on mutual expectations especially when it comes to mutual support
- Develop an action plan that includes ongoing one-on-one interaction
- Share mutual feedback as you go as to how stakeholders are responding

COMMUNICATION TIPS
if you are a Participator/Relater

PARTICIPATOR interacting with a:	Dos	Don'ts	Maximizing your impact as a PARTICIPATOR
TASKMASTER	Speak/Write in Bullets Agree on task Priorities Define People's Roles Focus on Results	Overload on Feelings Socialize too much Be Politically Correct Be Easily Offended	Let the Taskmaster be in Control Agree Action Plans & Follow-Up Steps Agree on Who is Involved Agree on how People will be Treated
ANALYZER	Share Facts/Details Agree on Priorities Develop an Action Plan Do One Step at a Time	Be Touchy-feely Ignore Key Details Be too Dependent Assume	Show the Analyzer your Competencies Define Who, What, When, Where, How Set and Update Goals and Steps Agree on Roles and Expectations
PARTICIPATOR	Identify the Customer(s) Share Feelings/Needs Customer Satisfaction Be Timely	Overload on Feelings Procrastinate Commiserate Miss Key Task Steps	Encourage the Participator to Share Focus on Customer Satisfaction Implement a Joint Action Plan Follow-Up in Person Often
ENERGIZER	Define Desired Outcome Stretch Outside the Box Respond Fairly Quickly Be Enthusiastic/Positive	Be too Personal Be too Sensitive Agree to Bad Ideas Be Overwhelmed	Praise the Energizer's Unique Abilities Agree on Customer Priorities Focus on Simple/Basic Steps First Agree on Who Does What Follow-Up Frequently in Person
FLEXIBLE *Taskmaster* *Analyzer* *Participator* *Energizer*	Limit Alternatives Get Focused Early Define Mutual Needs Manage Change	Be too Flexible Be Indecisive Be Hard to Read Wait too Long to Make Decisions	Determine Flexible's Current DNA Confirm Priorities Continually Define Conditions Constantly Check in Frequently Stick to Mutual Goals

FIGURE 15

CHAPTER 14
ENERGIZER/INNOVATOR

"Never speak of yourself to others; make them talk about themselves instead; therein lies the whole art of pleasing. Everybody knows it, and everyone forgets it."
— Edmond and Jules De Goncourt

The Energizer/Innovators comprise 20 percent of the normal population and tend to be the most visible of all the communication languages. Our Energizer/Innovator contributor is Mike Freeman the President of the Americas for WD-40. Here are Mike's thoughts about his communication language, his defining moments, his most impactful relationships and his perspective on Servant Listening:

"STICKY" WORDS AND PHRASES FROM MY ENERGIZER/INNOVATOR COMMUNICATION PROFILE

- **"...prefer working at a fast pace while you juggle multiple priorities and relationships"** – I love working with people doing activities that provide variety, low structure, challenge, creative opportunities and rewards. Doing the same thing every day in a highly structured environment with lots of rules or inflexible procedures is stifling, boring and unrewarding.
- **"...you give a lot and expect a lot in return"** As much as possible, if you do not enjoy what you do or have a passion for it, why do it?
- **"...you see rules merely as guidelines for action"** This is true within the context of being a law abiding, ethical and faith based person.
- **"...you enjoy coaching, mentoring and training when trainees are responsive, show initiative and are enthusiastic"** Coaching is one of my four key values expressed in my Leadership Point of View and is demonstrated through my passion

71

for teaching and working with Jr. and Sr. High School youth over the years.

- **"…is people, situations and activities, which move at a slow pace and which involve excessive detail and 'hands on' maintenance."** One letter response to this scenario……….. Z-Z-Z-Z-Z-Z-Z-Z-Z-Z-Z-Z

- **"…you focus on innovative strategies that can be implemented quickly with immediate results. Those around you may not completely understand what you have in mind because you tend to move from thought to action very quickly as stress increases."** If everyone else had my exact same education, experiences, insights, values, etc. everything I said and did would make perfect sense. Unfortunately, this is not the case and I need to remember that to minimize the chance of this happening, especially as a leader.

DEFINING MOMENTS

1. **Travel:** I took two trips of roughly 3-4 months each that impacted me as a listener:

After graduating from San Diego State University with a degree in American Literature and minor in P.E. and before beginning my work to get a teaching credential, I spent roughly 4 months travelling across the USA with my sister Kathy and next door neighbor Cathy. We went all over the USA and eastern Canada visiting family and friends fully exploring and experiencing this huge beautiful country of ours. During the trip, I decided to change my life direction and not teach literature and coach water polo and swimming at local high schools but to get my Masters in Business Administration instead.

The MBA degree I later received from SDSU in 1979 directly led to being hired by the IT department at a local ship building company named National Steel and Shipbuilding Company (NASSCO). I lived right on the beach and enjoyed the single life for a few years. Having discovered my country I now decided to explore the world starting with Europe. I quit my job, gave up my beach apartment, paid off my bills and took the remaining cash and went backpacking through Europe from September through December 1982 determined not to return home until the money was gone. I succeeded on all counts. I lived "Dr. John's France experience" in many countries while meeting incredible people of all nationalities, languages, experiences and opportunities. Like my previous grand exploration, I went into the trip thinking my return career would be working in IT for a San Diego company. Instead, when I returned I started a graphic design company with a good friend with no start up money (decision was made over a beer in Paris) because I always wanted to be an entrepreneur and thought I would like graphic design even better than IT.

Meeting the variety of people on these trips, hearing their life stories and different points of view, experiencing the languages and cultures, etc. all helped me expand my horizons, become more open minded, understand the opportunities we have here in the USA, recognize some of my listening "filters" and biases and become a better listener as a result. I was beginning to discover how to listen and enjoy differences in people rather than judge or dismiss them.

2. Family – Getting married and having kids:

Up until I met my wife DeeAnn, I was pretty set on living life my way with all the listening skills that lifestyle typically generates. Meeting and marrying DeeAnn changed that orientation and provided another lifelong "Listening Growth Opportunity" or LGO-1. I was not interested in having kids at the beginning of our marriage but over time we had three incredible children named Jay, Zach and Hannah providing LGO-2, LGO-3 and LGO-4 respectively. They have stretched me beyond myself over the years and helped me realize life is not about me but others. A major part of that realization is that I needed to start listening to them (and others) to be the husband/father I wanted to be. I wish I would have had the list of the seven transformational listening habits outlined in this book then. I could have progressed faster and earlier. I would love to tell you that after twenty-seven years of marriage and a thirty plus year work career that I have finally become a successful Servant Listener but there are too many witnesses among my family, friends and workplace that would say otherwise! This is a lifelong learning adventure and daily challenge.

INFLUENTIAL LISTENERS IN MY LIFE

1. Mr. Grimes – For three years starting in seventh grade I took piano lessons from a professional piano player who was an elderly and gentle teacher named Mr. Grimes. He amazed me with his listening skills in two ways. First, I could play any note or combination of two to three notes on the piano and he would immediately tell me what they were with his back to the piano and me. I realized then and even more now that this great listening skill was something he had trained for and practiced over many years. Becoming a Servant Listener will require all of us to follow his example of dedication and practice over time.

    Mr. Grimes saw early on that I got pretty bored taking traditional piano lessons. My playing skill was much better than my sight reading skill so he got very creative and changed how he taught me. Now he was listening to me with more than his ears! He spent 15 minutes each lesson doing traditional sight reading lessons. The last 15 minutes (or longer if I could get away with it) he played music at his professional level and I memorized what he did a few measures at a time. This not only helped ignite my passion for playing the piano and music in general but exposed me to the enjoyment of playing music from the 1940's, ragtime, boogie woogie, early rock and roll, the blues and so on. I still play many of those songs today.

2. My second listening influence (and I am doing theses in chronological order) is my wife DeeAnn. I am very good at listening with my head and she is great at listening with her heart (too). I hear the words; she hears all the facial expressions, body language, verbal tones, silences and other things that go along with the words. I listen with a bend towards facts and logic and she listens to things I do not perceive and fully appreciate (She sees spectrums of light beyond my narrow vision when communicating or listening.). As my LGO-1 (see above), I will spend the rest of my life trying to listen as well as DeeAnn typically does.

RADICAL LISTENING AT HOME AND WORK

I do not remember making a conscious decision on this but for much of my life I have led and listened somewhat differently at work than at home. A year ago I started to work on a Master of Science in Executive Leadership (MSEL) degree at USD with the support of the WD-40 Company. Ken and Margie Blanchard teach a class there about developing your Leadership Point of View. One of the many benefits of doing this is that the Leadership Point of View you develop is not just for the business world but also applies to leadership in all areas including family, neighborhood, church, etc. This integration of leadership in all areas has been a powerful and wonderful thing to understand and experience. I am currently experimenting with the idea of having one integrated approach to listening at work, home and everywhere else I interact with other people. My goal is to be a better listener and leader everywhere. I will let you know how the experiment works out in Dr. John's sequel to this book!

MY DESCRIPTION OF A RADICAL SERVANT LISTENER

I think to be a great Servant Listener and leader you have to do the following:

- **Work at it.** Like in sports or playing a musical instrument you need to consistently practice or the rust comes in (and WD-40 won't help you here). Remember perfect practice makes perfect.
- **Listen with humility.** I loved the definition of "humility" by Fred Smith in You And Your Network which says "People with humility don't deny their power: they just recognize that it passes through them, not from them." What a wonderful insight this provides about

where our real power comes from which should not be positional power (very often at least). If we are listening from a positional power location we will typically miss much of what is said (or not).

- **Practice flexibility.** Listen to everyone as much as possible (but exercise discernment when making decisions).
- **Overcome misperceptions.** A common mistake for a leader is to think "once a leader, always a leader." This thinking can result in people thinking they need to lead every group they participate in. Similarly, I think it is a mistake for us to think "once a speaker, always a speaker." There are times to speak but more times when we should be listening.
- **Listen with the intent of being influenced.** In the MSEL program we learn as leaders to "speak our truth" and "listen with the intent of being influenced." This is easy to say but very hard to do consistently.

If I had to define Servant Listening in a phrase I would go with **"listening with the intention of being influenced."**

RECOGNIZING AND RESPONDING

As you will see in Fig. 16, you can recognize the Energizer/Innovator because they will be very visible and active with their stimulating ideas and conspicuously poor listening. The Energizer/Innovator tends to experience pleasure with fast movement, change, exploration of the new and different and thinking outside the box. The EI tends to experience pain and discomfort with deliberateness, details for details' sake, standardization, bureaucracy and/or anything that unduly limits freedom and autonomy. The EI enjoys being the center of attention or having his/her ideas being discussed with a view toward implementation.

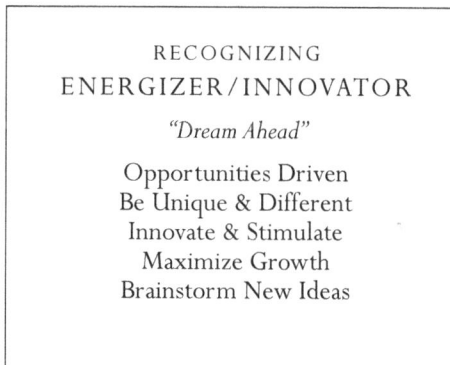

RECOGNIZING
ENERGIZER/INNOVATOR

"Dream Ahead"

Opportunities Driven
Be Unique & Different
Innovate & Stimulate
Maximize Growth
Brainstorm New Ideas

FIGURE 16

You can crack the Energizer/Innovator's Listening Code by using selective but sincere enthusiasm. Let them control the airwaves as much as possible. Periodically ask probing and focusing questions as you attempt to understand their vision and dreams. Ask them for specific examples of what they are proposing. Get caught up in their passion but realize that their energies are continually shifting back to the most exciting opportunities on their horizon. See Fig. 17 below for hints on how to respond effectively.

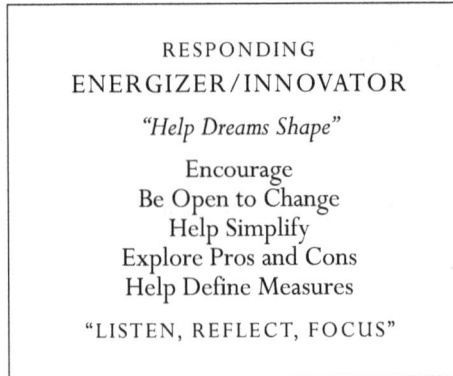

RESPONDING
ENERGIZER/INNOVATOR

"Help Dreams Shape"

Encourage
Be Open to Change
Help Simplify
Explore Pros and Cons
Help Define Measures

"LISTEN, REFLECT, FOCUS"

FIGURE 17

Listening Tips for the Energizer/Innovator are summarized below. Communication Dos and Don'ts are summarized in Fig. 18 (page 74).

RADICAL LISTENING WHEN INTERACTING WITH AN ENERGIZER/INNOVATOR

- Active and passionate attention to your Energizer is a must
- Listen for Blue Sky as well as for "here and now"
- Probe for the Energizer's specific expectations in general and of you
- Identify credible stakeholders and where they stand on the issue
- Help the Energizer to identify and focus on the most important factors
- Identify potential barriers and use a problem solving process
- Work out any concerns by starting with what you mutually agree
- Ask to summarize key points and then clarify
- Help Energizer not to marginalize issues and tasks
- Develop an action plan that is SMART (Specific/Measurable/ Attainable/Relevant/Timely)
- Give each other continual written verbal and written updates when things change. The Energizer will make changes and forget to tell you
- Keep an even keel as the Energizer oscillates up and down

COMMUNICATION TIPS
if you are an Energizer/Relator

ENERGIZER interacting with a:	Dos	Don'ts	Maximizing your impact as an ENERGIZER
TASKMASTER	Speak/Write in Bullets Agree on Task Priorities Be Creative & Practical Implement Action Plans	Lead with Wild Ideas Be too Conceptual Marginalize Basics Talk too Much	Reflect Taskmaster's Needs State your Needs/Ideas in Bullets Create Win-Win Solutions Implement Follow-Up Steps
ANALYZER	Share Specifics/Details Agree on Task Priorities Develop Plan Steps Do your Part as Agreed	Change without Buy-In Avoid Necessary Data Be Impatient Assume Anything	Define Who, What, When, Where, and How Be Creative yet Focused Agree on Plan Steps/Process Do your Part & Update Regularly
PARTICIPATOR	Identify the Customer Share Feelings/Needs Focus on Key Needs Include Key People	Overwhelm with Ideas Marginalize Facts Be Condescending Be Impatient	Focus on Customer Satisfaction Relate Actions to Benefits Be Low Key and Other Oriented Measure & Take Corrective Action
ENERGIZER	Co-Define Outcome Stretch Outside the Box KISS Be Enthusiastic	Be too Grandiose Be a Know-It-All Be Competitive Be Impractical	Brainstorm then Focus on Basics Agree on Who Does What Develop and Implement Action Plans Follow-Up and Make Corrections Often
FLEXIBLE *Taskmaster* *Analyzer* *Participator* *Energizer*	Limit Alternatives Get Focused Early Define Mutual Needs Manage Change	Be too Creative Be too Conceptual Avoid Tough Choices Wait too Long to Make Decisions	Determine Flexible's Current DNA Always Work Towards Mutual Priorities Reaffirm the Goal at Every Benchmark Check In and Stress Accountability Model Kept Promises

FIGURE 18

CHAPTER 15
FLEXIBLE/ADAPTER

"Life is a place of service. Joy can be real only if people look upon their life as a service and have a definite object in life outside themselves and their personal happiness."
— *Leo Tolstoy*

The FLEXIBLE/ADAPTER comprises about 15 percent of the normal population and is easily recognized because Flexible Adaptors continually change behavior based on the situation and people involved. Our example of the Flexible/Adapter is Ken Blanchard, the Chief Spiritual Officer of The Ken Blanchard Companies. Ken is a prolific speaker and author having penned *The One Minute Manager* with Spencer Johnson, *Raving Fans* with Sheldon Bowles, *Leadership by the Book* with Phil Hodges and Bill Hybels and many more. Ken is also the cofounder of the Center for FaithWalk Leadership. Not surprisingly Ken is also the creator of the Situational Leadership® II process.

Here are some excerpts from a recent interview with Ken:

Servant Leadership is the integration of leadership vision casting and followership action taking. The Servant Leader needs to first make sure that those around him or her are going in the right direction. The process of creating this vision and the goals and roles that follow is where the servant leader becomes a servant listener. The servant leader turns the leadership pyramid upside down to encourage all team members to do their unique best by giving them as much of the credit as possible. Each team member needs to be managed based upon their specific role, their related competencies and their respective communication language.

In my own life, my dad and several other early mentors were great servant listeners. Each of them made me feel as if I were the most important person in their world at the time. My dad especially was interested in whatever I had to say. He would stay focused on me when I was speaking, literally sitting on the edge of his seat. Years ago I met the Dalai Lama. To my surprise this learned man listened to me like my dad did — on the edge of his seat, hanging on my every word as if it were the last words he would ever hear.

I believe you can tell the servant listener in two ways:

1) How does he/she receive feedback?
   a. The Natural Listener tends to want to take credit or fix blame. His/her behavior tends to be reactive, defensive and non-affirming.
   b. The Servant Listener on the other hand wants to understand how best to serve others and welcomes honest feedback. His or her behavior is responsive, thankful and affirming.

2) How does a Servant Leader sort responses? My friend Tony Robbins once shared a perspective that has really stuck with me. He believes that when we listen and then eventually speak how we respond or "sort" separates the pretenders from the real listeners:
   a. The pretenders "sort" by taking a comment, topic or input from others and making it their own. They tend to relate it to their own experiences, values and perspectives. Their focus is clearly "selfish" whether that is their conscious intention or not. They take the ball away from the speaker and run with it themselves.
   b. The exceptional listener on the other hand "sorts" differently by probing and involving the speaker more and more in the topic. Their focus is "selfless" as they dig deeper and deeper into the ideas, needs and expectations of the speaker. Using the ball carrier example, the exceptional (servant) listener becomes a "blocking back" clearing the way for the speaker to continue running with the ball until they hit "pay dirt."

"The adventure of life is to learn. The purpose of life is to grow. The nature of life is to change. The challenge of life is to overcome. The essence of life is to care. The opportunity of like is to serve. The secret of life is to dare. The spice of life is to befriend. The beauty of life is to give."
— *William Arthur Ward*

RECOGNIZING AND RESPONDING

The Flexible/Adapter described in the Fig. 19, tends to experience pleasure with wide variety, multiple options, and passionate hanging on to simultaneous courses of action. Flexibles love to keep as many options open for as long as possible. The FA tends to experience pain when pinned down prematurely and/or with extremes including protracted task work, intense people interactions, exceedingly slow pace or chaotic activity.

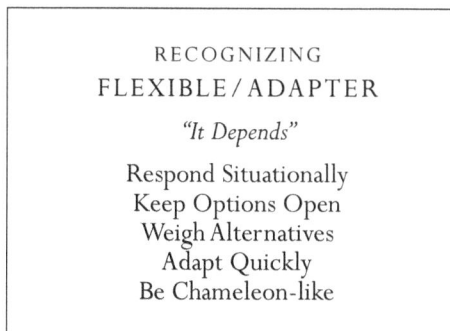

RECOGNIZING
FLEXIBLE/ADAPTER

"It Depends"

Respond Situationally
Keep Options Open
Weigh Alternatives
Adapt Quickly
Be Chameleon-like

FIGURE 19

If you want to crack the Flexible code see Fig. 20. Check in with them early and often to get a current "reading' on their position at that particular moment. Remember that Flexible's desire to be all things to all people at the same time. They live by the mantra "It Depends" so pin them down if you have to depend on them for anything.

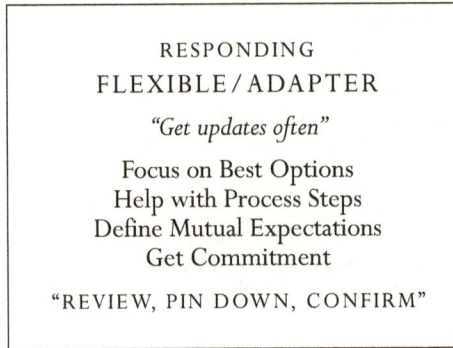

RESPONDING

FLEXIBLE / ADAPTER

"Get updates often"

Focus on Best Options
Help with Process Steps
Define Mutual Expectations
Get Commitment

"REVIEW, PIN DOWN, CONFIRM"

FIGURE 20

Listening Tips for the Flexible/Adapter are summarized below. Communication Dos and Don'ts are summarized in Fig. 21 (page 78).

RADICAL LISTENING WHEN INTERACTING WITH A FLEXIBLE / ADAPTER

- Open your mind and spirit to a wide variety of options
- Listen for the Flexible Adaptor's real concerns which will be masked in new alternatives
- Probe for required specifics and try to pin the FA down
- Identify the most credible options and stakeholders/suppliers
- Use reflective feedback early and often especially when the FA switches gears
- Identify and address problem areas using a systematic problem solving process
- When the FA switches gears and approach you need to re-establish mutual expectations
- Ask FA to limit options by picking out the best two and then comparing pros and cons
- Agree on your roles and the roles of others and readjust when the FA changes gears
- Develop an action planning process with discrete steps that are subject to change
- Give each other continual written and verbal feedback because things will be very dynamic

COMMUNICATION TIPS
if you are a Flexible/Adapter

FLEXIBLE *interacting with a:*	*Dos*	*Don'ts*	*Maximizing your impact* *as a* **FLEXIBLE**
TASKMASTER	Define and Clarify Get Common Language Pin Down Often Get Things in Writing	Be too Situational A Conditional Ally Marginalize Basics Flex too Much	Let the Taskmaster Take Control State your Needs/Ideas in Bullets Create Win-Win Solutions Implement Follow-Up Steps
ANALYZER	Share Specifics/Details Agree on Task Priorities Develop Plan Steps Do your Part as Agreed	Minimize Key Facts Avoid Specifics Be Impatient Spread too Thin	Respond to Analyzer's Need for Detail Be Creative yet Focused Agree on Plan Steps/Process Do your Part & Update Regularly
PARTICIPATOR	Identify the Customer Share Feelings/Needs Focus on Key Needs Include Key People	Avoid Interaction Ignore Signals Be Transactional Be Impersonal	Focus on Participator's Need to Socialize Relate Actions to Benefits Be Low Key and Others-Oriented Measure & Take Corrective Action
ENERGIZER	Co-Define Outcome Stretch Outside the Box KISS Be Enthusiastic	Be Non-Committal Juggle too many Balls Criticize Be Impractical	Praise the Energizer's Unique Abilities Agree on Who Does What Develop and Implement Action Plans Follow-Up and Make Corrections Often
FLEXIBLE *Taskmaster* *Analyzer* *Participator* *Energizer*	Limit Alternatives Get Focused Early Define Mutual Needs Manage Change	Be too Flexible Be Indecisive Be Hard to Read Wait too Long to Make Decisions	Determine Flexible's Current DNA Confirm Priorities Continually Define Conditions Constantly Check in Frequently Stick to Mutual Goals

FIGURE 21

CHAPTER 16
WALKING THE RADICAL LISTENING TALK

"Our unique gifting is never more unique than when we are using it to serve some-one else."
— *P. John Brunstetter Ph.D.*

THE OYSTER

"There once was an oyster whose story I tell,
who found that some sand had got into his shell.
It was only a grain, but it gave him great pain
for oysters have feelings although they're so plain.
Now, did he berate the harsh workings of fate
that brought him to such a deplorable state?
Did he curse at the government, cry for election,
and claim that the sea should have given him protection?
No- he said to himself as he lay on a shell,
since I cannot remove it I shall try to improve it.
Now the years have rolled around,
as the years always do.
And he came to his ultimate destiny: stew.
And the small grain of sand
that had bothered him so
was a beautiful pearl
all richly aglow.
Now the tale has a moral,
for isn't it grand
what an oyster can do
with a morsel of sand?
What couldn't we do
if we'd only begin
with some of the things
that get under our skin?"

Anonymous

JUST ONE MORE THING

This book is a labor of love and my humble attempt to share with you my failures and successes as a recent member of "Listeners Anonymous." My Vision is for you to stop the poor listening virus in its tracks in every relationship in your life. Begin transforming every relationship in your life using radical servant listening. My mission is to share with you what I have learned about overcomingthe most subtle, misunderstood and under-appreciated human failings that have undermined relationships. I suspect that you now agree that all of us have unfinished business when it comes to improving our listening behavior. We share a common bond as fellow sojourners in our quest to make a meaningful difference in others' lives and to leave a legacy of service. My humble wish is that you will make this book a treasured "pearl" as you transform you and every relationship in your life using radical servant listening.

Here is what I would like you to remember. You have the potential to become a radical servant listener if you are willing to let some sand get under your shell i.e., your ego. You need to be willing to endure the pain to achieve the gain. Unfortunately there are no shortcuts. Your natural DNA to be self determined and self fulfilled is a very powerful force with years of reinforcement. Constructive feedback on your listening behavior is an example of sand under your shell. Without it you are merely a legend in your own mind and "pearl less" oyster.

Our never ending challenge with becoming a radical servant listener is that the same nature that makes us self directed also makes us self centered and self serving. We talk the talk of being a more effective "difference maker." Our nature however, makes us unwilling to walk the walk due to the pain associated with changing our listening behavior. We say we want the pearl but we settle for the small candy bar. Unknowingly we fall way short of our difference-making potential. By harnessing the power of radical servant listening we can overcome our natural self orientation that has our current millennial culture in a relationship headlock. Serving others before ourselves is radical indeed and not easy. Radical Servant Listening is a powerful antidote that communicates that we truly care about others more than ourselves. Here is where the no pain – no gain comes in. Without the pain of the sand under our self-serving ego we cannot transform our relationships into pearls. Over time the persistent radical servant listener can fashion a "pearl necklace" of caring relationships. Never is our uniqueness so valuable as when we use it to serve others as no one else can.

If you want to make a difference in others' lives then start your radical listening plan NOW!

1) Post the Radical Listeners' Pledge prominently to remind you of the basics
2) Celebrate your listening strengths but make others the star!

3) Begin working on the listening weakness that will be the easiest to master

4) Write down an affirmation for each weakness on index card(s) one at a time and post where you can reinforce your improvement plan

5) When you show improvement in one listening basic, celebrate your success

6) One at a time pick new weaknesses to master and repeat the process

7) Work with an accountability partner to help you master radical servant listening

8) At the end of each day read and reflect on the Radical Listeners' Pledge and how you fared that day.

WALKING THE RADICAL LISTENING TALK

The classic definition of insanity is "Doing the same things over and over again, expecting a different result." Well the time could not be better to change the relative insanity surrounding your underwhelming listening behavior. As you apply radical servant listening tools in all your relationships, I encourage you to keep a written journal to record your progress. Don't be discouraged if others around you are not as passionate about radical servant listening as you are. I strongly suggest you invite those closest to you to read this book. Then you can discuss how to partner with each of them in your then shared journey to make pearls out of sand. Complete the online Listening Assessment and the Communications DNA Profile referenced in the appendix and ask others to do the same. Ask for a Communications Language Match which overlaps your profile with another. The Match then gives you customized recommendations for maximizing each pearl relationship in the making.

Now is your chance to "walk the talk" of radical servant listening by applying what you have learned in this book. Sit back, buckle up and get ready for an exciting adventure into Radical Servant Listening with a humble and loving heart.

Grab some sand and start making some pearls!

"Listen. Do not have an opinion while you listen because frankly, your opinion doesn't hold much water outside of your universe. Just listen. Listen until their brain has been twisted like a dripping towel and what they have to say is all over the floor."
— *Hugh Elliott*

ABOUT THE AUTHOR

John Brunstetter, Ph.D. an Energizer/Innovator is the CEO (Chief Encouragement Officer) for Team Interplay LLC. "Dr. John" also teaches in the Masters of Counseling program at Liberty University. John has been an adjunct college professor for more than 30 years with The University of California, the University of San Francisco, California Polytechnic University, and Saddleback Community College.

One of John's long-term clients has been the Ken Blanchard Companies where he has served as a technology provider for almost 10 years. Working closely with Francisco Gomez in their Office of the Future, Dr. John has provided the automated version of the Spanish Communications DNA Profile to Blanchard's Latin American clients. In addition to serving many small to middle market companies over the past decade, Dr. John has been an Organizational Development (OD) Consultant to WD-40, Qualcomm and a variety of high-tech and manufacturing companies. Dr. John is also working to provide communications technology and training to The Stewardship Alliance, Ronald Blue and Company, Family Wealth Partners and other wealth planning companies. These organizations also use the communications technology to develop and grow relationships with internal staff and external clients.

Prior to his mid career Ph.D. in OD from The Fielding Graduate University, John held senior leadership positions with Fluor Corporation, Warner Lambert, and Firestone.

He has been active in professional development community serving as the President of The American Society for Training and Development (Orange County CA Chapter) and PIRA (Personnel and Industrial Relations Association).

John and his wife Carolyn reside in Charlotte NC and have 7 children and 14 grandchildren. Their daughters Teresa and Dana are continuing the family teaching tradition started by John's parents, "Doc" who taught at Columbia and NYU; and June who began teaching in primary education after receiving a Masters in Education in her late 60s. Daughter Teresa is a Chemistry professor at Saddleback Community College (Calif.) and expects to complete her Ph.D. in 2012. Dana who completes her Bachelor's degree in Primary Education from Liberty University (Va.) in December 2011 expects to be teaching professionally soon thereafter. Dana recently returned from a stimulating and empowering summer ESL training program she conducted for Chinese children in Hong Kong sponsored by the English Language Institute of China.

It Only Hurts When I Listen is Dr. John's first book and fulfillment of his promise to document for posterity many of the lessons he learned from hid dad and professional mentor "Doc."

KEY RELATIONSHIP MANAGER (KRM)©

PROCESS STEPS

1. Ask the person if they are willing to help you apply your new servant listening behaviors in your future interactions with them. If they say yes then go to Step 2, below. If they say no then ask if you can sit down with them informally and share some things you have learned.

2. In advance of meeting with them determine what you believe is their communication language or combination languages that they best respond to and use themselves. Don't tell them initially what you came up with. Plan to interact with them according to what you determine is their most comfortable communication language.

3. Meet with them and give them a quick review of what you have learned using the Bits and Bytes, and then review Chapter 10 in some detail.

4. Ask them to let you know what communication language or languages they prefer you use with them. Apply all the new listening habits as you interact.

5. Go to the Chapter that covers the Listening Language (s) they select. For example. If your partner picks Energizer/Innovator as his/her preference go to the Chapter 14 Energizer/Innovator.

6. Alternately read the first few pages of the chapter out loud. Go over the Recognize and Respond Figures. Then Go to the Do's and Don'ts matrix and review the Participator/Relater line (your communication language) from left to right. Highlight the suggested Do's and Don'ts that your partner agrees would work well with him/her.

7. Ask this person to read the book themselves. After they complete it discuss the listening habits that each of you struggle with the most.

Agree on ways to support one another so that you each grow in areas of listening that need improvement.

8. Reexamine the language he/she selected in Step 4 above to see if that is where they now see themselves. If not, go to the chapter that reflects their desired language and begin with Step 5 above. You can make updates and changes as you go.

9. Now reverse the process. In the case above you both would go to the Participator/Relater Chapter (your language) and review the Recognize and Respond figures and then the Energizer/Innovator line. Agree on Do's and Don'ts for your partner's interactions with you.

10. Begin using the servant listener habits with each other AND start applying the Do's and Don'ts you both agreed on. Write down your mutual Do's and Don'ts behaviors and make a copy for each to use for review and as a reminder.

11. Meet periodically to give each other feedback on what's working well and what needs to get better in your relationship and to help each other master the 21 Radical Servant Listening Behaviors. Make mid-course adjustments and new commitments as you begin to transform your Relationship.

PRODUCTS AND SERVICES AVAILABLE

Team Interplay (TI), LLC is a leader in team, team leader and team member communications and team building training. TI now provides team leader and team member learning and development, online or on-sight.

The INTRPLAY DNA Profile,© TI's core tool, has been used by more than 150,000 people since 1985. Other tools include: The 360 Listening Assessment,© The Communications Language Profile,© The DNA Relationship Match Profile© and the Key Relationship Manager.©

Team tools used to support team building activities include the TEAMATCH Profile,© The Team and Team Leader (360°) Effectiveness Surveys and the Employee Opinion Questionnaire an all employee attitude type survey using national norms as well company specific questions.

Family tools include the INTRPLAY DNA Profile Family Version,© The Family Relationship Match Profile© and The FAMILY MATCH Profile.©

INTRPLAY tools are based on Dr. Brunstetter's PhD research and action research over the last 25 years. Dr. John discovered that the most critical human performance variable holding task specific competency constant was the "chemistry" between the team leader and the team member. More importantly he discovered that leader-member chemistry can be measured and improved using training and technology. The positive implications of improved chemistry have been significant when applied to individual and team performance. As participants learn how to use their uniqueness and communication language they also experience increased interpersonal trust, openness and appreciation for true diversity.

Profiles, Training and coaching are facilitated done a cadre of certified INTRPLAY professionals worldwide. For more information please go to:

Team Interplay LLC
Phone: 704–989–6472
Email: info@teaminterplay.com
Web: www.itonlyhurtswhenilisten.com

ENDNOTES

1 Blanchard and Johnson, *The One Minute Manager* 1982 William Morrow and Company

2 Blanchard and Hodges, *The Servant Leader*, 2003 published by J. Countryman

3 www.hillconsultinggroup.org

4 www.finestquotes.com Quotes by Carl Rogers

5 Here's a sobering but not all that surprising stat: only a third of workers (31 percent) say they are engaged in their job, and 17 percent admit that they are actively disengaged. Frankly, after all we've heard about unhappy workers who are ready to bolt for another job as the economy improves, I'm surprised that these numbers aren't a lot worse. But that's what comes from a new study titled Employee Engagement Report 2011 by global consulting firm Blessing White

6 The number of Americans who reported being happy with their careers dropped to an all-time low – 45 percent – in a 2009 Conference Board survey that found people are more miserable than ever in nearly every aspect of their work lives. Job satisfaction in 2009 was down from 61 percent in 1987, the first year of the Conference Board survey, and it's a 4-point drop from 2008. Only 51 percent now find their jobs interesting – another low in the survey's 22 years. In 1987, nearly 70 percent said they were interested in their work.

7 Surveys show that up to half of all workers have a shaky, if not downright miserable, relationship with their supervisors. According to a Gallup poll, a bad relationship with the boss is the number one reason for quitting a job. Supervisor problems outpace all other areas of worker dissatisfaction, including salary, work hours or day-to-day duties. The Gallup report puts it emphatically, "Employees leave supervisors, not companies."

8 One of the latest reports about divorce was released this year by the National Center for Health Statistics (NCHS). It is based on a 1995 federal study of nearly 11,000 women ages 15-44. It predicted that one-third of new marriages among younger people will end in divorce within 10 years and 43 percent within 15 years.

9 1 to 1.5 million children run away from home each year. Somewhere between 20 and 40% (depending on where you live) will become involved

in high risk behavior including drug use, prostitution, pornography, or starvation on the streets. Approximately 50% of all runaway children do not believe social service agencies are helpful. According to the Federal Bureau of Investigation's National Crime Information Center (NCIC) there were 840,279 missing-person entries (adults and juveniles) in the year 2001. A review of NCIC data shows that approximately 85-90 percent of those entries were juveniles. Thus, in approximately 725,000 cases (or on average 2,000 per day) the disappearance of a child was serious enough that a parent called law enforcement and the law-enforcement agency took a report and entered it into NCIC. It should be noted, however, that the vast majority of these cases are resolved within hours.

[10] MetaAnalysis_Q12_WhitePaper_2009.pdf (377198 bytes)

[11] 1967 The Classic Film *Cool Hand Luke* starred Paul Neumann

[12] 2011 *Contagion* starred Matt Damon

[13] Doc shared his leadership training notes with me while he was The Global Leadership Development Guru for ITT Corporate. I was humbled to work with him for about 5 years in the twilight of his career and at the beginning of mine.

[14] Blanchard and Barrett, *Lead with LUV* 2010 Financial Times Press

[15] www.searchquotes.com/search/Karl_Menninger/

[16] http://www.wonderbabiesco.org/UserFiles/File/Graven%20and%20Browne%20Auditory%2008.pdf

[17] www.theodoreroosevelt.org/life/quotes.htm

[18] The phrase "Servant Leadership" was coined by Robert K. Greenleaf in *The Servant as Leader,* an essay that he first published in 1970.

[19] Blanchard and Hodges, *The Servant Leader*, 2003 published by J Countryman

[20] Blanchard, Ken Convene (February 1998) p75.

[21] www.hillconsultinggroup.org

[22] www.goodreads.com/author/quotes/838305.Mother_Teresa

[23] www.quotationspage.com/quotes/Anais_Nin

[24] www.miltonsdb.org/LinkClick.aspx?fileticket=D...tabid=78

[25] www.searchquotes.com/quotes/author/Carrie_Fisher/

[26] www.motivatingquotes.com/briantracy.htm

[27] www.quotationspage.com/quotes/Hugh_Elliott/

[28] www.blog.gaiam.com/quotes/authors/robert-greenleaf

[29] www.searchquotes.com/quotes/author/Catherine_Ponder/

[30] William Shakespeare: Hamlet Act 3, scene 2.

[31] www.quotationspage.com/quotes/Walt_Whitman

[32] www.goodreads.com/author/quotes/47352.Federico_Fellini

[33] http://www.kenblanchard.com/Issues_Organizational_Development/Effective_Leadership_Solutions/One_to_One_Talent_Management/Management_Situational_Leadership_Training/

[34] Chapman, Gary, *The Five Love Languages* 2004 Northfield Publications

[35] http://thinkexist.com/quotesbyletter/jof%20jor/

[36] www.jkrishnamurti.org/

[37] www.quotationspage.com/quotes/William_Arthur_Ward